MEDIA CULTURE SOCIETY

A SOUTH ASIAN READER

EDITORS : DR. SAYAN DEY & DR. V RATNAMALA

Contents

Preface

In the 21 st century, global communication has ushered in plethora of possibilities and phenomenon to galore. It is not only dismantling the political, economic, cultural and technological boundaries but also merging the media, both traditional and advanced, into binaries. Politically, the global communication is transcending national borders by broadcasting foreign news, entertainment, educational, and advertising programs with impunity (example- Direct Broadcast Satellite (DBS).

Phenomenons like micro-media, narrowcasting, new media and social media have become the new buzz words in political engagements. On economic front, distinct industries which were built around these technologies have become combined to cater to the multimedia environment through corporate alliances and mergers. Culturally, the implications are widespread with concepts of global pop culture, cocacolonisation, McDonaldisation among others. Commodity fetishism is at its peak, courtesy global entertainment and advertising industry. In addition, global communication is empowering hitherto forgotten groups and voices in the international community. Its channels have thus become the arena for contestation of new economic, political, and cultural boundaries. Global communication, particularly in its interactive forms, has created immense new moral spaces for exploring new communities of affinity rather than vicinity. It is thus challenging the traditional top-down economic, political, and cultural systems. Accelerating technological advances in telecommunications and their worldwide dissemination are profoundly changing the rules of international relations. Global communication is thus redefining power in world politics in ways that traditional theories of international relations have not yet seriously considered. Major changes seem to be taking place in both hard and soft power conceptions and calculations. Although no grand theoretical generalizations on the dynamics of hard and soft power are yet possible, trends indicate that the latter is assuming increasing importance.

At this juncture this edited volume attempts to encapsulate the essence of 21 st century International communication, its scope and prospects. Further, the provocative compilation envisages creating a platform to engage and re-engage into the most pressing issues and notions in the domain of post-colonial global communication.

Editors
November 7, 2022

About The Editors

Dr.V.Ratnamala is a Professor in the Department of Mass Communication, Mizoram University, Aizawl, Mizoram, India. She was a Visiting Fellow at Institute for Comparative Modernities, Cornell University, Ithaca, New York during Feb-May 2020. She is also the coordinator for Technology Enabling Centre at Mizoram University sponsored by Department of Science & Technology. She got her PhD from Manonmaniam Sundaranar University, Tirunelveli, Tamil nadu. Prior to join here, she has worked as lecturer in the department of Mass Communication, Manonmaniam Sundaranar University for three years. Her area of research is media coverage of Dalit issues. The title of her doctoral thesis is *"Dalit Issues and Tamil Press: The Coverage of Dalit Participation in Politics in the Southern Districts of Tamil Nadu"*.

Dr. Ratnamala has presented papers in the national and international conferences. She has also published research papers extensively. Her research interest includes media and Minorities, race, space and the city, science communication, media and conflict reporting and political economy of media. She is teaching theories of communication, advertising, research methodology, media and gender, radio production and Media, culture and society. She has successfully guided and awarded four PhD scholars and more than 50 Post graduate Dissertations.

She was the recipient of 'Young Scholar Award' from CPR South in 2014. She recently completed a Joint Research Project titled, "Race, Space and the city" under ICSSR (India) - NIHSS (South Africa) Joint Research Programme in Social Sciences. She collaborated with Prof. Rozena Maart, Director, Centre for Critical Research on Race and Identity, University of Kwazulu Natal, Durban, South Africa for that project.

Sayan Dey is an Assistant Professor at the Department of Mass Communication, Mizoram University. With over 8 years of teaching and research experience, he has published in indexed journals as well as contributed chapters/articles in books and edited volumes. He has also co-edited an edited volume on 'Media and Marginality : From Theory to Praxis'. He received his doctoral degree in the domain of New Media and Hybrid Culture. His research areas include Print Media, New Media and Digital Culture, Media and Gender among others.

CHAPTER ONE

The Effects of Social Media on Young Women's Intercultural Adaptation and Body Image Satisfaction

Ms. Aiswarya Thamanna[1], Dr. R. Subramani[2]
1. Research Scholar, Department of Journalism and Mass Communication, Periyar University, Salem, 636 011, Tamilnadu, India-Mail: aiswaryathamanna26@gmail.com
2. Associate Professor, Department of Journalism and Mass Communication, Periyar University, Salem, 636 011, Tamilnadu, India.erasubramani@gmail.com

Abstract

The importance of new social media in our daily lives has increased in today's culture of globalization. They provide an environment where people from all over the world may interact, communicate, and share knowledge without restriction. Social Media Promoting cross-cultural understanding entails giving information through interaction to enhance intercultural adaptation so that it leads to a new set of circumstances and provides adaptation to different cultures.

People frequently use social media to retain contacts and better blend into the host culture while adjusting. Body image is a multifaceted, dynamic construct that is influenced by both external cultural and social variables as well as interior biological and psychological ones. Our levels of individual body pleasure have been impacted by the evolving social and technical environment around our globe. The media is among the biggest contributors to the emergence of body image dissatisfaction. This study aims to examine how social media use affects young women's intercultural adaption and body image satisfaction.

In the Salem district of Tamil Nadu, 50 Young women were collected using a purposive sampling technique. The data gathered from an in-depth interview is examined using a constant comparative method. For this research, the Sociocultural theory anduses and gratification theory functioned as a theoretical framework for this study.

Key Words: social media, Women, Intercultural adaptation, Body Image satisfaction, Culture.

INTRODUCTION

Social Media Usage and Women

women use social media at comparable rates-For a number of years, women were more likely than men to utilize social networking sites, though these differences have subsequently become negligible. Today, 68% of all women and 62% of all males use social media.

The rapid transmission of news, text messages, video clips, and other information that a person would find helpful in his daily life was made possible by social networks like Facebook, Twitter, and YouTube (Rabeh, 2010). These networks act as platforms for establishing one's own personality and publishing oneself. Users of these platforms have access to the subjective worlds of others through the self-portraits and stories they provide on their personal profiles.

Intercultural Adaptation

Common characteristics of culture include things like ethnicity, sex, religion, nation, dialect, knowledge, profession, time, belonging, and status. These distinctions give rise to a separate sense of cultural identity and indicate various cultural social structures. civilizations all around the world value the particular traditions, beliefs, and norms that make them different, social media unites people from all over the world despite differences and geographic limits. As a result, culture, which can be defined as a society's way of life and includes things like how people see birth and death, is a crucial component of the social structure. It is quite challenging to define culture because it has so many different meanings. The first possibility is that culture is a social construct that each person builds over the course of his or her life. (Voronina, 2019).

Modern technological development has created new virtual spaces for interaction. These spaces are represented in social networks, which have transformed reality into circles full of daily developments and allowed for extensive and branching communication despite distances (Zemmouri, 2011). As a result, a new culture has emerged that differs from the culture of the traditional society, which is based on customs and traditions (Gates, 1998).

Today, the emergence of "global village" where people from many cultures may communicate. During intercultural adaptation, people use social media to learn about their host countries, establish and maintain contacts, and stay up to date on developments in their home countries. Communication and participation have a significant impact on social media's influence on intercultural adaptation (Rebecca Sawyer,2011)

Body Image Satisfaction

Body image is a complex, dynamic construct that is impacted by internal biological and psychological factors as well as external cultural and social factors. The Austrian psychiatrist Paul Ferdinand Schiller (1886–1940), who asserted that people's mental representations of their own bodies explain how they first encounter their bodies, initially suggested the idea of body image as a psychological phenomenon in 1935. The psychiatrist asserts that a person's view of their physical appearance is shaped by unconscious perceptions, ideas, and feelings. This representation is developed and reconstructed throughout life (Goswami et al,2012)

Since being thin is associated with beauty, which is desirable, society values it while strongly detesting its adversary, obesity. The ideas of female beauty vary depending on the esthetical standards established at each epoch, but studies show that women have tried to change their bodies to adapt to these norms.

REVIEW OF LITERATURE

Social media encourages cross-cultural engagement and affiliation within our global community, social media is significant in our lives. People can connect and communicate with information that is efficiently available on the Internet because of social interaction media. Social media is becoming more and more integrated into everyday plans and layouts as a result of the increasing number of Web users in today's culture. These online forums for communication encourage lively discussions that deepen knowledge of divergent points of view. Everyone on the internet is a publisher and a reviewer because social media sites like Facebook and Twitter let users share their ideas with the world and take part in debates on a single virtual platform (Georgetown University, 2010).

Many factors, especially for women, such as cultural beliefs, societal norms, physical changes to our bodies, and happenings in our behavior affect how we feel about our bodies (Bedford & Johnson, 2006). One of the most common reasons for body dissatisfaction is being aware of the expectations for perfection and appearance that society and our specific group of friends, coworkers, and peers hold (Myers & Crowther, 2009).

Because they don't feel satisfied with their lives and feel inadequate, they put themselves at a higher risk for depression and anxiety. The worst cases of discontent may substantially impair social, academic, and/or occupational functioning (Goswami et al, 2012).

Cultural differences have an impact on communication, behavior, and values. Based on national identification and gender, there are differences in how users of social networking sites (SNSs) who identify with various cultures govern their communicative behaviors (Rosen et. al, 2010).

According to Kohls, "psychological confusion most people experience when they move for an extended period of time into a culture unique from their own" is what is known as culture shock (2001). Intercultural adaptation causes culture shock in everyone, which might affect how they communicate and behave.

In a globalizing society, people from different cultures can only communicate effectively and productively if they possess global communication abilities (Chen & Starosta, 1996, 2005). It is essential to acquire cross-cultural communication skills in order to comprehend different cultures and communicate effectively in the modern world. Competence includes cognitive, affective, and behavioral traits in relation to the four elements of global communication competence—global thinking, unfolding the self, mapping the culture, and aligning the encounter (Chen, 2005). There are important factors that could facilitate or obstruct adaptation in an online situation, including host social communication and ethnic social communication (Chen, W., 2009). The social, physical, and cultural aspects of social media have an impact on intercultural adaptation.

RESEARCH QUESTIONS

- Does Social media usage by young women increase day by day?

- Does Social media usage reduced Stereotypic beliefs and prejudice towards other cultures among young women and whether intercultural adaptation is increasing among young women?

- Does negative belief in body image is increasing among young women?

- Does Young Women have dissatisfaction with their body image?

- Does body image satisfaction is reducing among young women?

THEORETICAL BACKGROUND

According to the tripartite impact model and sociocultural theory, family and peers are the two biggest factors on body dissatisfaction. According to theory, these three factors might affect body dissatisfaction directly as well as indirectly through social comparison and internalization of beauty standards (i.e., ideal of youth and thinness for women).According to the social comparison, people are compelled to evaluate themselves in a variety of fields, and if there are no objective ways to do so, they compare themselves to others. While it is not normal for people to constantly draw comparisons that are detrimental to their self-esteem (i.e., comparing themselves to those they feel to be better off than them), this is exactly what occurs when it comes to comparisons based on appearance. Even when these comparisons are unflattering, have a negative impact on their body image, or are made to irrelevant targets like professional models, women frequently make upward comparisons with their appearance (Samantha Stronge et al.,2015)

According to sociocultural theory, gives users the chance to compare themselves to others frequently and widely, which is bad for their bodies. Upward social comparison on Facebook has been linked longitudinally to body dissatisfaction, and social comparison has been found to mitigate the relationship between media exposure and body dissatisfaction generally (Samantha Stronge et al.,2015).

The basic premise of uses and gratifications

theory is that individuals will seek out media among competitors that fulfills their

needs and leads to ultimate gratifications (Lariscy et al., 2011).

The basic premise of uses and gratifications

theory is that individuals will seek out media among competitors that fulfills their

needs and leads to ultimate gratifications (Lariscy et al., 2011).

The basic premise of uses and gratifications

theory is that individuals will seek out media among competitors that fulfills their

needs and leads to ultimate gratifications (Lariscy et al., 2011).

The basic premise of uses and gratifications

theory is that individuals will seek out media among competitors that fulfills their

needs and leads to ultimate gratifications (Lariscy et al., 2011).

The basic premise of uses and gratifications

theory is that individuals will seek out media among competitors that fulfills their

needs and leads to ultimate gratifications (Lariscy et al., 2011).

The fundamental tenet of the uses and gratifications theory is that people will seek out media among rivals if it satisfies their wants and results in long-term gratifications. (Lariscy, R.W., Tinkham, S.F. and Sweetser, K. D,2011). The personal and social roles and routines of media consumers will undergo significant change if the Internet proves to be the technological marvel that many believe it to be. (Quarterman & Carl-Mitchell, 1993).

RESEARCH METHODOLGY

The qualitative research comprised in-depth interviews. The constant comparative method of data analysis allowed flexibility to generate themes meaningful for the study. The study was conducted in the Salem district of Tamilnadu. A purposive sampling technique was used to select young women who use social media to know their intercultural adaptation and body image satisfaction. The study was conducted among 50 young women and In-depth interviews were used to collect data. All young women who participated in this study were college-going students and everyone who has been using social media for a while.

Interviews lasted around 30 min, were conducted in the local language Tamil, and took place on the participant's campus. After a depth Individual interview, each question asked during individual interviews focused on individual freedom for using social media Apps to find out social media usage patterns in their daily life, the influence of social media usage on intercultural adaptation, and body image satisfaction. During the individual interviews, participants were asked about their individual social media use and their views on body image dissatisfaction and cultural adaptation as an individual. In-depth interviews were audio recorded and transcribed later for analysis.During the interview, these are the questions asked them to collect data.

Are you using social media? Consider Facebook, Twitter, YouTube, Instagram, and WhatsApp. How often? How much time?

Why do you live a life that includes social media? How long do you typically spend on social media usually?

Do you think your capacity to adapt to various cultures has improved as a result of utilizing social media?

Do you think social media has helped you get over stereotypes or prejudices about your culture while educating yourself about others' cultures?

What part does social media play in making you feel a part of both your own culture and the society you're visiting or familiar with through social media?

Do you think social media has increased body image dissatisfaction as a result of social media usage?

Do you think social media has decreased body image satisfaction while watching the girl's images and videos?

DATA ANALYSIS

In the analysis part in-depth interview conducted among 50 young women, and data were analyzed through constant comparative method to reach conclusion.Through comparative method data is analyzed to know the social media usage among young women, their intercultural adaptation and body image satisfaction. To support the analysis some of the Responses is added here in the analysis part.

Social Media Usage Among Young Women

Participants involved in the study are using social media. They used Facebook, Twitter, WhatsApp, YouTube, LinkedIn, and Instagram. Most of the participants use social networking sites multiple times a day, and some log in weekly to communicate with friends and family. A few sites are checked a couple of times a month just to get updates and check the news.

I've been using social media to communicate with my family and friends last three years"(p27). I use WhatsApp instead more than Facebook because I feel more convenient(P40). A lot of Women who are studying also use this one, and I probably use WhatsApp more than Facebook because a lot of my friends back who have it" (P9). I have profiles on well-known websites like Facebook, Instagram, and WhatsApp, although I spend more time on WhatsApp and Instagram than on Facebook. I log in many times a day for a total of around an hour (P21). When discussing how much time I spent on social media, I used to spend a minimum of 45 minutes per day on

WhatsApp, on average. I spend more time on it when I am chatting with my friends" (P1).

We were able to gain information about other people's activities, but I felt like I was aimlessly wasting time on social media. It would be best if you balanced how much time you spend on social media sites and you can't rely solely on social media when building relationships" (P2). "From my perspective, communicating with people who reside outside of my own country is made easier by using social media" (P10).

The participants of my study used social media sites to communicate with their friends and family and to stay in touch with people with whom they cannot spend time face to face. Staying connected to people is important for relationships in order to maintain contact and connection. social media sites are used not only for maintaining contacts and building relations but also to share information, news articles, photos, resources, and links. people who were using social media sites varied; some participants were more passive with interacting online, while others were very active users who communicated frequently.

Personally, I use WhatsApp to talk to my family, but I post photos and videos. (P7). I don't interact much on social media but I observe there are many people who update and post interesting content and videos, mostly I just observe these things and people in my network (P6). "When I don't have time to meet up in person, I use social media to keep in touch with people. I also use social media to keep in touch and be updated with my friends and family. I probably use social media more to stay connected with people back in my native place" (P8).

Expressing opinion freely: All participants said that their free expression of their opinion had increased in light of their use of social media. All respondents reported that their discussion of issues and events with colleagues and friends had increased in light of their use of social media. Half of the respondents stated that their friendship with people from other countries and states had increased in light of their use of social media.

Face-to-Face Interaction: Many of the respondents stated that their eagerness to talk with the family had decreased in light of their use of social media while they are in the same shelter.

negative effects of social media, the respondents shared were wasting time and inability to organize daily activities, the development of laziness and lethargy among individuals, then weakens direct in face-to-face communication skills, falsification of information, and then addiction to its use by day by day.

it helps in searching for cultural and religious matters, searching for job opportunities, Online Purchasing, and paying bills electronically easily it is a good way to have fun and spend time than developing skills and displaying talents to others to prove oneself.

Intercultural Adaptation Among Young Women

The component of language and method of dialog with others is one of the difficulties to adapt to other languages. It can be difficult to comprehend a language other than our own. I spent a lot of time watching videos because I couldn't understand anything from the videos from another language while watching first time on social media (P35). I think social media helped me because after watching those videos, I started talking to people more confidently and I came to know the differences, so I became adjusted to the culture. I would have to say YouTube helped me, from the language perspective, learn the short, slang words and shortcuts, especially when people post things on their walls" (P3).

"Social media has provided me with a means by which I have been able to better learn other languages, in my opinion. From the cultural perspective, I saw a lot of pictures on Facebook, which illustrated what life was like in other cultures" (P19).

Most of the Respondent's said that taking into account speaking and writing in a spoken language and interest in correcting linguistic errors had decreased in light of their use of social media. Many of the respondents said that using colloquial language in conversation with others increased. The use of new and common terms and use of new and circulating words among young women has increased in light of their use of social media.

Thinking about traveling abroad and emigrating: Many of the women respondents said that their thinking about traveling abroad had increased due to getting addicted to photos and travel videos they are watched on social media. Cultural differences and everyday life, especially seen through photos of social events on social media helping to find out the cultural differences easily. Lastly, social media was used to help the students who are studying far away from their native place with the English language (English is commonly used language in mostly everywhere), especially the slang and common phrases. Because of how people are raised differently throughout cultures, there are significant differences in how social media is used.

Boundaries are thinning and this thinning of boundaries causes cultures to be more similar because of Westernization and modernization, so in this way, social networks and intercultural adaptation have grown (P11) people who wish to travel to another country or another state, social media is a good place to learn about the host culture, and I would recommend using social media, from my personal experience in getting better knowledge about other cultures" (p17)

I felt embarrassed because I didn't go to the places of other countries, but it's totally different food, clothes, the lifestyle here because it's more common for us to understand the way one dresses up, eats, and how independent the girls in other places are. It's not wrong and it's not right; it's just different. I'm able to know this because I looked at a lot of pictures on social media sites related to this. Their culture gives an entirely different way of life. I feel that if I was born there how I will be right now (P3)? Every generation adopts a distinctive culture, and every culture is distinct in its own right.

The way cultures use to adapt to lifestyles by people in their life is also different but they get a chance to know the cultural adaptation of others through social media "(p6).

Body Image Satisfaction among Young Women

Most of the Respondent's said that they are getting more beauty-related videos through social media and with the emergence of social media Apps filtering images is possible for all and it's not showing the actual skin color. Women are tending to believe that other women whom they are seeing photos and images on social media are fair and also project that skin texture is very smooth and glowing without normal body human hair. Many of the respondents said that using social media insist on beauty concepts in young women, primarily about fairness, body hair, shape, and weight. The young women who are not that fair, the one who have body hair is getting more body image dissatisfaction.

Many of the respondents revealed their dissatisfaction with their body image and some of the responses are, I watch videos and other entertaining content on social media. "I also use it to stay current on fashion trends and learn about beauty topics.

But every woman who is in the videos is very fair and they have smooth glowing skin without body hair. But I have body hair and my skin is not that fair and it is acne-prone skin. I feel dissatisfied a lot of times myself a lot regarding my body image. (P43)

women experience the perception that they are fat, they are also judging their bodies because they believe that the weight and shape of their bodies are important. Therefore, if a woman is experiencing feelings that they are overweight, they are also judging that their body and/or weight is undesirable.

I saw a lot of pictures of women on Instagram and YouTube, which show the lifestyle and habits others like in their cultures". The girls who are living in the city wear modern dress and its suits them well. But I am not getting a chance to wear a dress like that, suppose if I will get that kind of modern dress, it is not suited for me because I don't have a perfect body shape and I have belly fat (P32).

women who feel anxiety regarding their personal body image are less likely to experience the levels of happiness that are evident in women who do not experience concern about body image. if a woman feels there is a large discrepancy between her actual self and her ideal self, then the likelihood is that she will have stronger negative feelings about her body. "I keep an eye on the behaviors and portrayals of women in my network, their attire, cosmetics, accessories, etc. I'm a limited user of makeup and accessories but after watching photos and videos of women in my network and their changes in physical appearance I wondered and I compared myself with them. I felt dissatisfied myself because I'm not that fair, so makeup is not suited for me as well as accessories(P41)." According to this data, women who sense discrepancies between their actual and ideal selves are likely to also feel that they are overweight or "fat" at the same time.

According to literature evaluations, men often express less body dissatisfaction than women (Tiggemann 2004).

CONCLUSION

The results of this study emphasize the importance of social media usage on intercultural adaptation and body image satisfaction. From the participants' reports, one can infer that people strengthen, build, and maintain relationships through social media. The interactions and conversations establish interconnectedness, which is an important component for communicating with people in the host and home countries, and it establishes a sense of community. Understanding is an essential factor in intercultural adaptation, and social media influences this process. Before arriving at the host place the participants watch and sometimes talk about using some social media to become more familiar with the host place, they wish to be there once upon a time. To get to understand cultural norms and traditions also social media serve as a place for interaction and conversation in order to get in touch with contacts with peoples who are in other place and ask about the intercultural experience.

Social media help them to get information on the different points of view available to them, and simply being aware and recognizing the different impressions create a wider worldview perspective on cultures. Relationships and connections have an impact on a person's sense of community as they adjust to a new culture. After getting knowledge about other cultures women adapting other cultures in their lifestyle Specially Food items and dresses and cosmetic and beauty items Women adapt more to other cultures.

It created integration into the new culture, and social media contributed to this development. Simultaneously, social media provides an outlet where people have the opportunity to communicate with friends and family in order to stay updated, aware, and informed of current events. Participants spoke about how social media helps them feel like they are still part of their home country and they are started using the English language more in their daily life conversations and short informal words from other languages too.

The recognition that younger women have negative self-beliefs about their body image, especially regarding their body weight, shape and skin color, and body hair, these exposures can prove detrimental to physical and mental health that relate directly back to body esteem is apparent.

Strong messages of body acceptance and self-love, particularly to young women and adolescent girls, can assist in reducing the impact of intercultural shock and societal norms that getting through social media and its impact expounding what is expected of females in terms of weight management, skin color body shape.

LIMITATIONS

There were several ways in which this investigation was constrained. However, these restrictions point to a direction for further investigation. First, due to time constraints, I only interviewed 50 young women who were college-going students. Interviewing a larger number of students or expanding to other places across the country would be beneficial in creating a greater understanding of my research. In addition, the majority of the interviewees studying in college have been taken from the Salem district of Tamilnadu. For further research, Women students from a wider range of countries around the world could be interviewed in order to gain a broader perspective of social media and intercultural adaptation and body image satisfaction from a more diverse population. Also, the age range of the participants could be expanded to include more people, and not just those adjusting to college life. Older and younger generations could be studied.

IMPLICATIONS FOR FUTURE STUDY

Future studies can expand on body image satisfaction among all age of women and also men. social media and intercultural adaptation among both men and women also could be a study area.

Social media usage is increasing rapidly, it would be relevant to understandamong which gender, body image satisfaction and intercultural adaptation is very high. What is the role of social media and other factors affecting, intercultural adaptation and body image satisfaction.

REFERENCE

- *Cash, T.F. and Pruzinsky, T.E. (1990). Body Images: Development, Deviance, and Change. Guilford Press, New York.*
- *Bedford, J. L., & Johnson, C. S. (2006). Societal influences on body image dissatisfaction in younger and older women. Journal of Women and Aging, 18, 41-55.*
- *Chen, G.M., & Starosta, W.J. (2005). Foundations of intercultural communication. Lanham, MD: University Press of America.*
- *Goswami, et al. (2014). Body image satisfaction. Industrial Psychiatry Journal.*
- *Gates, B (1998). Informatics after the Internet—the way to the future" (trans: AA-S Radwan). The World of Knowledge, Kuwait, p. 231.*
- *Kohls, L.R. (2001). Survival kit for overseas living. Yarmouth, ME: Intercultural Press.*
- *Lariscy, R.W., Tinkham, S.F. and Sweetser, K.D. (2011), "Kids these days: examining differencesin political Uses and Gratifications, internet political participation, political informationefficacy, and cynicism on the basis of age", American Behavioral Scientist, Vol. 55 No. 6, pp. 749-764.*
- *Myers, T. A., & Crowther, J. H. (2009). Social comparison as a predictor of body satisfaction: A meta-analytic review. Journal of Abnormal Psychology, 4, 683 – 698.*
- *Quarterman, J.S., &CarlMitchell, S. (1993). Thecomputingparadigm shift.Journal of Organizational Computing, 3, 31–50.*
- *Rabeh A-S (2010). Digital identity and youth: between social representations and self-representation. International Forum on Youth, Communication and Media, Research Unit in Information and Communication Technology, Institute of Journalism and News Sciences and Konrad Adenauer Foundation, Tunisia.*

- *Rogers, E. (1995). Diffusion of Innovations, New York: The Free Press.*
- *Rosen, D., Stefanone, M. A., &Lackaff, D. (2010). Online and offline social networks: Investigating culturally-specific behavior and satisfaction. In Proceedings of the 43rd Hawai`i International Conference on System Sciences. New Brunswick: Institute of Electrical and Electronics Engineers, Inc. (IEEE).*
- *Slade, PD. (1994). What is body image? Behav. Res Ther, 32:497-502.*
- *Sawyer, R. (2011). The Impact of New social media on Intercultural Adaptation. Senior Honors Projects, Paper 242.*
- *Veltri, N.F., &Elgarah, W. (2009). The role of national cultural differences in user adoption of social networking. Paper presented at the Southern Association for Information Systems Conference, Charleston, SC.*
- *Voronina, O.A. (2019). Philosophical thought, vol 7 https://nbpublish.com.*
- *Wardle J, Bindra R, Fairclough B, Westcombe A. (1993). Culture and body image: Body perception and weight concern in young Asian and Caucasian British women. J Community Appl Soc Psychol,173-81.*
- *Zemmouri, ZBK. (2011). The emotional relationship between the sexes using electronic means between the virtual community and the real community. J Humanit Soc Sci 2(6):189–23.*

CHAPTER TWO

News: Globalizing the Local and Localizing the Global

B. Uday Kumar
Ph.D., Scholar
Department of Electronic Media And Mass Communication,
Pondicherry University, wiseant7@Gmail.Com
Dr. Nivedhitha Devadas
Associate Professor
Department of Electronic Media And Mass Communication,
Pondicherry University, nivedhithadas@Gmail.Com

Abstract

Recently the dynamics of news broadcasting on local television channels have changed,following the rapid increase in the internet penetration, Indian audience have access to numerous international news portals. Global news has become easily accessible. Local news channels have started to broadcast the news with global appeal in order to meet their audience's needs. News dissemination has extended to every nook and corner of the world and is now capable of reaching its target audience that are dispersed across the world, with the help of mobile gadgets and various electronic devices with the help of internet services. With the help of internet, local audience are exposed to international affairs. This has been facilitated by many media like Movies, social media and various other channels. This has created an interest in the localaudience about international events and news.

This study will investigate how local news grabs global attention and what kind of local news is gaining international appeal. Also, the way global news is getting localized with more regional flavors and hyperlocal content. It will adopt textual analysis methods to delimit and analyze the news contents within the online news portals.

Keywords: News, Globalization, Localization, Internet, Consumers.

Introduction:

In India, television broadcast began on 15th September 1959, based on a pilot experiment. The actual daily broadcast began six years later, in 1965 with aim of broadcast development at the village level (Singhal & Rogers 2001). SITE (Satellite Instructional Television Experiment) was the first initial step in the direction of satellite television in India. Indian television history can be studied by dividing it into two parts. Firstly, before the liberalization of the Indian economy and secondly, post-liberalization of the Indian economy. In 1976, Indian television history had seen a significantmilestone as *Doorsharshan* was established as a distinct body and separated from All India Radio (Page and Crawley, 2001). Since then, *Doordarshan* started a substantial increase of entertainment programs that include films, serial and dance sequences, songs, and coverage of sports besides commercial advertisements and news bulletin. The first commercial program aired on *Doordarshan*was *Humlog* (we people). During the tenure ofIndira Gandhi as a Prime Minster of India, in 1982, the broadcast of the ninth Asian Games created a significant landmark in the history of Indian television as it was broadcasted programs in a colour format.

India made advancements in satellite technology a range of INSAT(Indan National SATillite) launched. By 1988, the access of television received 62 per cent of the population (Singhal & Rogers 2001,85). During, P.V. Narasimha Rao's Prime Ministerial ship 1990-1991, the government of India had adopted the New Economic Policy whichhas enabled the entry of private and foreignbroadcasters in India. Since then television programming especially in news broadcasting gradually changed by inviting foreign media entities. The introduction of private channels such as Star TV and Zee TV in 1991- 92, escalated Indian media with competition and Since then, Indian media became part of the Global world. As of 28th February 2022, according to MIB,the total number of permitted channels including news and current affairs is902.

In India, Internet services was introduced in 1995 by Videsh Sanchar Nigah Limited (VSNL). Till 1999, the Internet penetration in India was 0.1 per cent and increased to 11.4 percent in 2012 as Airtel introduced 4G services in the same economic year. As the Reliance Industries introduced the Jio serves with rock-bottom prices and focused on mobile data consumption, and the availability of Smartphones in the market at a low cost to common. It has brought the average data usage per month gone up to 14.1GB in 2022, from 1.6 GB in 2017, according to the Economic Survey of India 2022.

This phenomenon escalated the consumer's usage of digital media more than conventional media. The content, especially news either local or international is easily accessible to consumers over their smartphones. Accessing foreign news channels, movies, and other entertainment content became at a distance of fingertip. As the viewers are receiving international news content on their handheld gadgets, television broadcasters were forced to have exclusive news bulletins about international affairs, in their programs in order to meet their audience requirements and consequently increase their viewership. Global content is being transformed into local content such as "who wants to be a millionaire". In the late nineteen and early twenties, only the formats of the global television programs had been adopted and Indianized by adding Indian elements or involving local actors or iconic figures as globalization refers to the increased global relationships between nations based on culture, people, technology and economic activity

How the local news content is appealing to an international audience. Similarly, how the international content is being localized. What are the elements and consequences that are making news global to local and Local to global.

The Rationale of the Study:

Globalization process started with 16th-century geographical explorations, followed by colonization and the cold war (Kumar & Welz 2003). Marshal McLuhan called the world a 'global village' in his work Understanding Media (1964). This world has become a global village in terms of culture, trade, and education with the help of improved technology. Most of the scholarly work has been donein social science in the field of culture, films, gender language, print ,electronic media, and News media and how technology helped the world to become globalized. But how globalization is taking place in news broadcasting has been neglected. There is a void in this area. This paper will try to fill the gap.

Research Objectives:

1. To understand how the local content is being globalized in satellite television news broadcast, and global content is being localized.
2. To examine what kind of news content is being 'globalized', localized.

Research Questions:

1. What kind of local news ishaving international appealing?
2. Why are they happening?

Methodology:

The purpose of textual analysis is to describe the content, structure, and functions of the messages contained in texts. Textual analysis is all about a text. What is text in the textual analysis? The main aspect of the textual analysis is to become familiar with the concept of a "text". Literary and visual constructs, employing symbolic means, shaped rules, conventions and traditions intrinsic to the use of language in its widest sense (Hall, 1975:17). In the qualitative research method, we frequently refer to the text to articulate more than an inscribed document, textbook, or cellphone message. Usually, we make meanings from texts. A text can not only be a written peace but also includes various types of texts like -books, films, pictures, newspapers, magazines, websites, games, television programs, radio broadcasts, advertisements, fashion, and popular music, etc.

All the examples of texts can be interpreted by the researchers, relating them to media, culture, and society.

However, it is not only interpretation but also to examine and to draw a key line of the text by considering the surface meanings and underlying intentions of a text. As the goal of textual analysis is be to bring out the entire range of potential meanings in the texts.

As the textual analysis method is the appropriate technique to deconstruct the television messages, it is incorporated in this study and analyzed selected news bulletins from variousregional and international news channels for a week and analyzed in this study.

Analysis and Findings.

In this study, three television news channels - one is from the International news channel -'Al Jazeera' and another two were local news broadcasting channel 'Sakhi TV' and TV9 news channels have been selected for this study. From each channel news programs like 'NRI news bulletin from Sakshi channel, and "START HERE" news bulletin from 'Al Jazeera' channel eventually "Prime Time news bulletin" from TV9 have been selected as a research study. From these news channels a week-longnews bulletinin the month of September have been studied in-depth. Textual analysis method has been incorporated to deconstruct to analyze andto understand the news, which comes under the qualitative research Methodology.

Sakshi TV is a Telugu News Television channel that was launched by Indira Television Limited Group in erstwhile Andhra Pradeshon 1st March 2009headquartered in Hyderabad which has shifted to Vijayawada now. It is basically a 24X7 news and current affairs channel also broadcasts news related to sports, music, film, and business, andhas coverage in both Telugu-speaking states. It reports ground-level news within the region in the local language. It started a news bulletin called 'NRI' (Non-Resident Indian), aweek-long news bulletin that has been taken as a sample from this channel.

The NRI news bulletin reports news, from both Telugu speaking states Telangana and Andhra Pradesh about politics and some other local interesting events. This program is targeting Telugu NRI audience who are spread across the world especially in America and European countries.

In one of the bulletins NRI program broadcasted a news has been broadcasted about group of students studying in government high school who are able to speak English with American accent in Bengal Pudi village of Kakinada District of Andhra Pradesh. A student named Meghana from this school is bright student and speaks fluent English with American accent. Thesestudent were given a chance to meet speak with the Chief Minister of Andhra Pradesh. They showcased their English skills Infront of Andhra Pradesh Chief Minister. This was broadcasted in various local news channels including Sakshi. The same news was also broadcasted in NRI edition which gained the attention of NRI community.

An NRI social media activist Hari Krishna has come forward to help Meghana to achieve her goal as she wants to become a Doctor in her career. He also criticized the social media trollers who were demoralizing Meghana on social media.

Similarly, another student Reshma from the same Benda Pudi government high school imbibed the American accent was also featured in the episode. An NRI named – Prabhakar who migrated to America from Andhra Pradesh, came to know this news through Digital media and extended his support to the Benda Pudi government high school by offering a library facility.

The school head master had appreciated the progress made by the students with the help of their English teacher and has plans to upgrade the school with more facilities with help of government and NRIs like Prabhakar.

This local news, which was broadcasted on Sakhi TV under NRI news bulletin had grabbed the attention of the NRIs living in various foreign countries. This NRIs, had come forward to extend their support these students.

This is an example of how local content that was broadcasted in local news channel, is being globalized through the digital media. Digital media is a space where both local content and global is bringing together and is being transformed them according to consumers interest from local to global or global to local. This new phenomenon is being termed as 'glocal' or 'glocalization' by the scholars.

Whereas, another television channel that was selected for this study was 'Al Jazeera'. Itis an international English news with 24X7 news broadcasting channel headquaterted in Doha, Qatar. It was launched on 15th November 2016, has a full coverage of the Middle East and it was the first English news channel in the Middle Esast region.The channel had anticipated to reach out 40 million households bur it covered 80 million houses. It started a news bulletin "START HERE" where anchor Sandra Gathmann presents stories.

According to Al Jazeera's portal, 'START HERE' is a program which combines journalism with innovation in the digital space. It telecasts new programs every week and this program meets the needs of sophisticated digital audience – an audience that demand quality and speed. Its unique content is driven by the stories that have people talking about the issues.

According to Al Jazeera this program doesn't have any hype or agenda nor any gimmicks but, quality production and journalism that gives people what they need to form their own views. It employs graphic designing, picture editing and visual representation of data to the audience.

START HERE news bulletin was analyzed for seven days and following observation are mad. Each episode is fifteen minutes long.

In one such episode which was analyzed, had a news item of Queen Elizabeth's death.Anchor Sandra talks about Queen Elizabeth's death and its impact on British empire and how it has gained people's attention, talking about the British empire. She also explains about the changes that were introduced by the queen during her reign. All this was presented in a narrative way.

In the same bulletin, there was a news item about Taliban takeover of the power in Afghanistan following the withdrawal of American troops. Sandra reads about Afghanistan's political situation. Thousands of Afghanis were desperate to leave the country,with the fear of the Taliban's rule.

In anotherepisode, Sandra comes up with Lebanon's cost of living crisis.How the Lebanese citizens are facing soaring inflation, as the cost of living changestheirway of life.

With these news items START HERE is making itself appealing to the global audience as it is a global television channel, its target audienceis global consumers.

Sample:

Sakshi TV

September 2022

S No	Date	Length of the video in Minutes
1	24/09/2022	20:48
2	25/09/2022	19:36
3	26/09/2022	13:28
4	27/09/2022	20:03
5	28/09/2022	19:00
6	2909/2022	23:50
7	30/09/2022	21:23
8	Total	116:40

TV9 Telugu

September 2022

S No	Date	Length of the video in Minutes
1	24/09/2022	NA
2	25/09/2022	15:19
3	26/09/2022	04:13
4	27/09/2022	15:49
5	28/09/2022	12:42
6	29/09/2022	16:49
7	30/09/2022	16:38
8	Total	80:10

Al Jazeera

S No	Date	Length of the video in Minutes
1	24/09/2022	11:37
2	25/09/2022	NA
3	26/09/2022	NA
4	27/09/2022	NA
5	28/09/2022	12/27
6	29/09/2022	11:57
7	30/09/2022	29:15
8	Total	64:36

TV 9 Telugu is a 24X7 news broadcasting and current affairs channel, which was launched in January 2004 in Hyderabad as its headquarter, in Telangana, India. It was launched by Ravi Prakash. It also broadcasts news in other Indian Languages like Bangla, Kannada, Tamil, Gujarat and Marathi. It broadcasts the news in different segments like Sports news, Film news, News Junction, Metro news, village news, and National news, both Telugu-speakingstates news. Prime time news bulletin is being broadcastedat 9 PM. In the broadcasting arena, this time frame 9 PM news on television is being considered significant. People after reaching their homes from the workplace and while having their dinner watch the prime time news to know what happened in the whole day around the world.In TV9 channel, the prime-time news bulletin has been taken as a sample for a week and investigated international news coverage.

In TV9 channel, prime time news bulletin has varioussegments. News Junction-segment has broadcasted the news item about China's PresidentXi Jing Ping. There was a piece of fake news about China's President on social media in China as if "he was house arrested" which became viral.This international news from China was broadcasted in local televisionnews by adding the local flavor to itsaying from China to Chile social media iswhistling about China's President Xi Jing Ping that he was house arrested. This is how global news is being localized by adding local elements.

Conclusion:

Since India has opened up its market to the rest of the world with its liberalizationpolicy in the 1990s, the Indian media landscape has been changed. Foreign Direct Investment (FDI) had got increased in the field of media. Many foreign entities and Indian private television channels had come up. Since 2008, when smartphones reached to the common man ata reasonable price the usage of the Internet through mobile phones had increased in India. In 2016 Reliance Industries introduced the Jio 4G services with rock-bottom prices and focused on mobile data consumption. This has brought a dramatic change among Digital media users. All the content which is produced by traditional broadcasting news channels got accessible through mobile internet as well. As the mobile internet enabled consumers to access international news contentand entertainment programs over their smartphones, television news channels started to broadcast to international content even inlocal channels in order to keep their viewership. In this process, local television channels are broadcasting international news content by adding local elements to that content and localizing them.

In this regard, three television channels have been selected for this study and investigated one news program on each channel for approximately a total of four hours. Due to time constraints, one-week programs have been investigated in each channel and analyzed how local content isattracting the global audience, the elements involved. Similarly, how international news content is also being localized. Future researchers can take more channels as a study population to investigate this phenomenon further. This paper will help as a reference for further research.

References:

Aravind, Singhal & Everett M. Rogers (1989). *'India's communication revolution; from bullock cart to cyber marts.'* Detroit, SAGE publications.

Bonnie S. Brennen (2013). *'Qualitative Research Methods for Media Studies'* by Routledge.

Castell.M (2000). *The Rise of the Network Society,* 2nd edn. Oxford: Blackwell.

Desai.M.K (2017). *Indian Television in the Era of Globalisation: Unity,Diversity or Disparity?*

Joyappa, Deepak & Rodrigues, Usha & Rani, Dr. Padma. (2020). *"The Internet's Potential: A Study of Indian News Sites."*

Meenakshi.S (2015). *"An Vital Analysis of Effect of Globalization on Indian Television and Culture in a Present Scenario".*

Sunethra, Sen Narayan (2014). *'Globalization and Television; a study of the Indian Experience 1990-2000'* New Delhi, Oxford University Press.

Thussu D. Kishan (2007). *'News as entertainment; the rise of global infotainment.'* Los Angels, SAGE publications

https://www.trai.gov.in/sites/default/files/PR_No.02of2022.pdf
https://www.indiabudget.gov.in/economicsurvey/
https://www.youtube.com/watch?v=RAKrkPV5zSs
https://www.youtube.com/watch?v=h-YVbjOBW38
https://www.youtube.com/watch?v=Xrl0FXCVN8k
https://www.youtube.com/watch?v=rnB3aSCc3PQ
https://www.youtube.com/watch?v=7h6t7iRBGXE
https://www.youtube.com/watch?v=PSwvWfQ26O0
https://www.youtube.com/watch?v=qUQ9iFgtJYY&t=3s
https://www.youtube.com/watch?v=q5z0yRf68FI&t=27s
https://www.youtube.com/watch?v=hX6CzNW2E_4
https://www.youtube.com/watch?v=bN9Da0mLsF8
https://www.youtube.com/watch?v=06d7lh7tA6o
https://www.youtube.com/watch?v=u5aguYx3rDs&t=432s
https://www.youtube.com/watch?v=CObIwrN-Es8

CHAPTER THREE

Effects of Web-Series among College Going Students

Ms. Harithaa M
Assistant Professor
PG and Research Department of Visual Communication
Holy Cross College, Tamil Nadu
E-mail – harithamohan.1@gmail.com

Introduction

The world is becoming interconnected because of the higher internet usage. Internet usage in India in current phase is rapid and it is shaping the individuals in social, cultural and attitudes wise.Madhukalya (2020), has studied on the increasing of online consumption during the Covid-19. It has increased to 13% from 9% in daily average consumption. During the Covid 19 lockdown phase the students are more into the gadgets as they had online education. Online Education brought the gadgets to students with free access for longer time without any restriction. Choudhary (2020), has made study on impact of Covid19 on educational sectors in India. During this period internet acts as a blessing and e-learning comes as a definite solution to make the education system on. Both students and teachers are connected with each other and share knowledge from their own destinations. Though it is a blessing students used the internet and gadgets for entertainment like watching online video contents specially the web-series. Web- series is series of scripted or non-scripted online videos, generally in episodic form, released on the Internet. Unlike the Television soap operas where people should can watch only an episode a day, the Web -series paves way to watch collection of episodes at a stretch without any time restriction and break. This pulled the youngsters towards the web-series. The interesting cliff-hangers in the end of the episodes made them binge watch the series. Binge watching means watching two or more episodes continuously without break. The web-series are available in various Over-the-Top (OTT) platforms in India like Netflix, Disney+ Hot star, Zee5, Sony Liv, Amazon Prime etc., all the OTT platforms has web-series of different languages and different countries. The new story line from regular soap operas attracted the students towards web-series. This research focuses on the effects of watching web-series among college going students.

Literature Review

The digital revolution in India is largely driven by smart phone penetration, the roll out of 4G, reducing data costs and thereby increasing time spent on mobile phones. Digital advertising is thus expected grow at a faster clip as against the traditional media over the next three years.

An upsurge in the usage of smartphones in India has stirred a new era of video consumption on the personal media device. The penetration of smartphones in India is projected to grow to 520mn by 2020 and broadband penetration will increase from 14% currently to 40% in 2020. (Ernst & Young, 2016). This increase will be instrumental in aextreme shift of media consumption from traditional to digital. There has been a decline in the percentage of Indian Consumers who prefer watching shows on TV from 47% to 10% over the last one year. (Accenture, 2015).

Numerous studies have proven direct or indirect effects of binge-watching web series and online streaming content on the youth. Research by Sung, et al (2005) suggested that binge behaviours are thought to be closely related to negative feelings. Many studies provided examples of research articles that provide correlation between binge watching, body dissatisfaction, academic loss, bleak symptoms and low esteem.

Netflix binge Scale (2016) reports, instead of one episode per week, Netflix members choose to binge watch their way through a series - that is, on average, finishing an entire season in one week. Binge watching is clearly the new normal, not all series are enjoyed.

Peterson Theodore (2016) examined the effects of binge-watching on social and academic lives of college students, where he stated, "For many participants, the rhythm of their day was built around binge-watching. The scheduled a time to binge-watch web series and awarded themselves after their activities. While the participants downplayed or were unaware of the effects of this new watching experience, their grades suffered, their social lives are ignored, and the schedule is determined to an extent by their binge-watching habit.

Research Question

What motivates the students to watch web-series?

What effect do web series have on how young people are perceived?

What effects do web series have on young people's behaviour?

Objectives of the Study

To investigate how young people in India perceive web series

To learn the reasons behind the behavioural alterations in young people brought on by their web series addiction.

To find out the impact of web series on the academic performance of the youth.

Methodology

The respondentsfor this study were the undergraduate college going students from Chennai and Tiruchirappalli. The age group of the students are from 17 – 22. The sample size was 100. A questionnaire was prepared to collect data from the respondents. The questionnaire contained options for answers with four or five-points on the Likert scale. The SPSS software was used for findings and analysis of the data.

Findings and Analysis

Frequency Test:

Fig.1 says 55% of the students always and often prefer mobile to watch Web-Series. 32% of the students prefer sometimes and rarely. Only 13% of the students never watch Web-series using the mobile phone.

Fig. 1

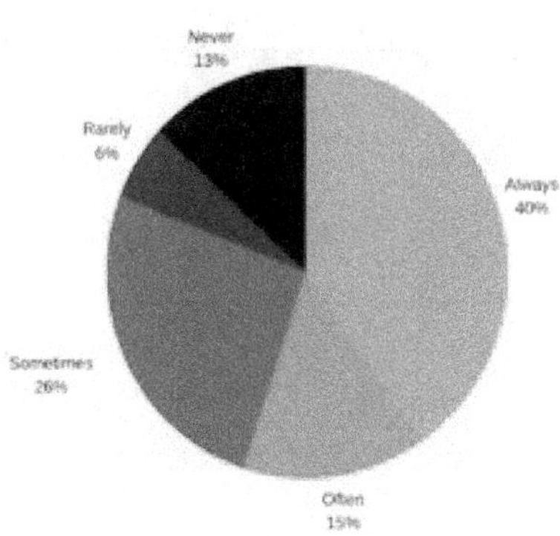

Fig.2

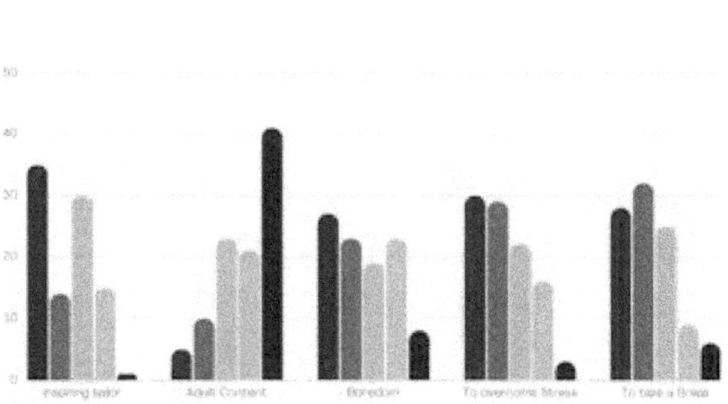

Fig. 2 explains things that motivates to watch web-series.

49% of the students always and often gets inspired by the trailer to watch web-series.

41% of the students sometimes and rarely motivated by the adult content shown in the web-series.

50% of the students watch web-series always and often as they are bored.

59% of the students watch web-series always and often to overcome stress.

60% of the students watch web-series always and often to take a break from their regular activities.

Table: 1 One-Way ANOVA

S. No	Dependent variable	F value	Sig. value	Degrees of freedom Between groups (df)	Degrees of freedom Within groups (df)
1	Watching web-series made me feel Lonely	5.540	.005	2	98
2	Watching web-series made me feel Excited	3.554	.032	2	98
3	Affects Academic Performance	3.940	.023	2	98
4	Affects Sleep	4.339	.016	2	98
5	Changed Dressing Style as shown in Web series	4.358	.015	2	98
6	Changed Hair style as shown in Web series	5.013	.008	2	98

One-way ANOVA was done with the independent variable "Average hours spent watching we-series in a day" which was recoded as "Exposure to Web-series" with three groups namely Light Viewers, Moderate viewers and Heavy Viewers with different dependant variables given below.

The students who watch web-series from half an hour to 1 hour in a day are classified as Light Viewers; those who watch web-series from 2-3 hours are classified as Moderate viewers and more than 4 hours are classified as Heavy Viewers. The Test yielded a significant result.

Table: 2 Post Hoc Test

S.No.	Dependent Variable	Light Viewers	Moderate Viewers	Heavy Viewers
1	Watching web-series made me feel Lonely	4.00	3.35	4.18
2	Watching web-series made me feel Excited	2.23	2.86	3.69
3	Affects Academic Performance	2.26	2.92	3.64
4	Affects Sleep	2.62	3.04	3.32
5	Changed Dressing Style as shown in Web series	2.86	3.95	3.02
6	Tried Hair style as shown in Web series	2.95	3.29	3.91

1. Watching Web-series makes me feel Lonely as the Dependant variable and Exposure to Web-series is significant.

$F(2,100) = 5.540; p =.005$

The Post-Hoc test was done where the Heavy viewers(M=4.18) feel most lonely that Light viewers (M= 4.00) and Moderate Viewers(M= 3.35).

The heavy viewers are spending most of their time in watching web-series that makes the separated from the actual world and that makes them feel lonely than the moderate viewers and light viewers.

2.Watching web-series made me feel Excited as the Dependant variable and Exposure to Web-series is significant

$F(2,100) = 3.554; p=.032$

The Post-Hoc test was done where the Heavy Viewers (M= 3.69) excited to watch a Web-series than the Moderate Viewers (M= 2.86) and Light Viewers (M=2.23).

The uncertainty in events and the interesting content of the web-series makes the heavy viewers highly excited than the moderate viewers and light viewers.

3.Watching web Series Affects Academic Performance as the Dependant variable and Exposure to Web-series is significant.

$F (2,100) = 3.940; p=.023$

The Post-Hoc test was done where mostly the Heavy viewers(M=3.64) academic performances are affected than the Moderate Viewers (M=2.92) and Light Viewers (M=2.26).

Concentration in web-series is high that spending most of the time in watching the web-series naturally affects the academic performance.

4.Watching web Affects Sleep as the Dependant variable and Exposure to Web-series is significant.

$F_{(2,100)} = 4.339; p=.016$

The Post-Hoc test was done where heavy viewers(M=3.32) sleep is getting affected mostly than the Moderate viewers(M=3.04) and Light Viewers (M=2.62).

5.Changed Dressing Style as shown in Web series as the Dependant variable and Exposure to Web-series is significant.

$F_{(2,100)} = 4.358; p=.015$

The Post-Hoc test was done where Moderate Viewers(M=3.95) changed their dressing style highly that the Heavy viewers(M=3.02) and Light Viewers(M=2.86).

6.Changed HairStyle as shown in Web series as the Dependant variable and Exposure to Web-series is significant.

$F_{(2,100)} = 5.013; p=.008$

The Post-Hoc test was done where Heavy viewers(M=3.91)changed their hairstyle mostly than the Moderate viewers(M=3.29) and Light viewers(M=2.95).

Discussion and Conclusion

The study shows that most of the students use mobile phones to watch web-series.As the mobile phones are always with them and the unrestricted time, unlimited internet with mobile phone, privacy, mobility makes the student to use mobile phone always to watch a web-series. Trailers refer to short previews of a video content, these are common for movies and web-series. These trailers will be promoted in the social media websites are highly inspired by the students to watch a web-series. There is a minimal effect on the adult content shown in the web-series, this proves that students watch web-series for the interesting contents of the web-series more than only for the adult content.

Most of the students watch web-series as they are bored or to take a break from their daily deeds, but binge-watching behaviour makes them to forget their regular duties. More than half of the students started to watch web-series to overcome stress. The heavy viewers can be termed as binge-watchers, the test results of Analysis of Variance show heavy exposure to web-series have adverse effect on the student's attitudes and behaviour. The heavy viewers feel lonely as they spend most of their time in watching we-series. Their interest is watching web-series and when some they see new trailers of web-series they are highly excited. When the avoid many regular activities, they also ignore studies which naturally affects the academic performance of the students.

The students are changing their dressing style and hair style as shown in the web-series, which says that the students want to portray themselves as their favourite characters. Slowly the students' attitudes and behaviours are changing according to the web-series that they watch.

References

1. *Accenture. (2015). Digital Video & the connected consumer. Accenture. Retrieved on 15th September 2022*

    https://www.accenture.com/_acnmedia/Accenture /ConversionAssets/ Microsites/Documents17/Accenture-Digital-Video-Connected-Consumer.pdf

2. *Choudhary, R. (2020). "COVID-19 Pandemic: Impact and Strategies for education sector in India", ET-Government. Retrieved on 12th July 2022*

    https://government.economictimes.indiatimes.com/news/ education/ covid-19-pandemic-impact-and-strategies-for-education-sector-in-india/ 75173099

3. *Ernst & Young, (2016)*
4. *Madhukalya, A. (2020). "India's Internet Consumption up during Covid-19 Lockdown, Shows Data". Retrieved from https:// www.hindustantimes.com/india-news/india-s-internetconsumption-up- during-covid-19-lockdown-shows-data/ story- ALcov1bP8uWYO9N2TbpPlK.html accessed on September 2022.*
5. *Netflix (2016), Netflix binge scale*

    https://about.netflix.com/en/news/netflix-binge-new-binge-scale-reveals- tv-series-we-devour-and-those-we-savor-1 - Retrieved on 5th October 2022.

6. *Peterson Theodore (2016) to binge or not to binge: A qualitative analysis of college students' binge-watching habits.*
7. *Stickney MI, Miltenberger RG, Wolff G (1999) A descriptive analysis of factors contributing to binge eating. J Behav There Exp Psychiatry*

8. *Vinod S. Koravi, "Analysis of various effects of web series streaming online on internet on Indian youth", International Journal for Research Under Literal.*

9. *Pawan Singh Malik (2021), Psychosocial Impact of Web Series and Streaming Content: A Study on Indian Youth, Global Media Journal.*

   https://www.globalmediajournal.com/open-access/psychosocial-impact-of-web-series-and-streaming-content-a-study-on-indian-youth.php?aid=90530 Retrieved on 21ˢᵗ October 2022

10. *Pramit Gupta (2021), THE FACTORS EFFECTING SHIFT OF INDIAN CUSTOMERS FROM TV SERIES TO WEB SERIES- THE FUTURE OF OTT SERVICES IN INDIA, EPRA International Journal of Multidisciplinary Research (IJMR)*

   https://eprajournals.com/jpanel/upload/ 1014am_IJMR%20FEB%202021%20FULL%20JOURNAL.pdf#page=150 Retrieved on 20ᵗʰ October 2022

An Impact Study on the Effect of Whatsapp Political Memes on Marginalised Youth Of Thiruvannamalai Towards Their Political Affiliation

Infant Kingsley A
P.G. and Research Department of Visual Communication
Holy Cross College, Tamil Nadu
kingsleysj@gmail.com
Dr Arul Selvi
Head and Assistant Professor
P.G. and Research Department of Visual Communication
Holy Cross College, Tamil Nadu
arulselviselvi@hcctrichy.ac.inselvimagar@gmail.com

Scheme of the paper

The advent of the internet has caused huge impact upon digital platform such as Social Media. It has created a big impact upon the people on political sphere. By way of new communication technology, it has reshaped media and politics. Today it can be addressed as hybrid media system. It is a new concept that considers the ever-changing relationship between media and politics. It integrates the roles played by old and new media focusing in their interactions (Chadwick, 2013). Such a system has evolved as one of the powerful and impact- oriented political communication. Researches address various perspectives of the association between Social Media and politics. Today people, especially youth feel so very comfortable with the prominent hybrid media with a compulsive visual culture. The contemporary condition is often described as a state of being surrounded, even bombarded by images. The condition is also characterized as an image flow, increasing in its intensity as the means and sources of image production and distribution continue to expand all around. Pictures are said to be the most common way of spreading information, of making an impact, of expressing oneself, of influencing others (Karin Becker, 2004). The vast majority of rural and marginalized youth are no exception to such an association which can easily motivate or de-motivate them in taking decision. The social media content such as WhatsApp political memes (SyedSaad, 2021) which is very widespread among the youth can influence their decisions pertaining to their political affiliation. Often times the influence of Whatsapp political memes do reflect in their choice of voting in electoral politics.

Thus youth being the maximum users of social media, the aim of this study is to critically analyze the impact caused by WhatsApp political memes on the selected group of marginalized youth who live in Thiruvannamalai, one of the most backward districts of Tamil Nadu through a sample survey. This study also aims at addressing the impact of social media content and how it influences the youth in the selected study area. The focus of the study is the role of WhatsApp political memes, their circulation of information towards constructing political knowledge and the voting pattern. This study can also lead to further exploration of the impact and influence of peoples" affiliation to a party and their voting pattern.

Key Words: WhatsApp, political memes, marginalized youth, political affiliation

Introduction

The advent of the internet has caused huge impact upon digital platform such as Social Media. It has created a big impact upon the people on political sphere. By way of new communication technology, it has reshaped media and politics. Today it can be addressed as hybrid media system which is a new concept that considers the ever-changing relationship between media and politics and integrates the roles played by old and new media focusing in their interactions (Chadwick, 2013). Such a system has evolved as one of the powerful and impact- oriented political communication. Researches address various perspectives of the association between Social Media and politics. A pervasive explosion of social media networking is the order of day. It has become the byword of the people especially the youth. It permeates in all spheres of life. It has redefined the axiom „Homosapien as homoconsumen" (man as a social animal to a consumer animal). Man is a social media monster" (RJ Parker, 2014). The proliferation of social networking sites (SNS) and social networking applications (SNA) have begun to control, determine, justify and perpetuate people"s practices, beliefs, convictions, emotions and other expressions in their day today life. In less than last five years (2020), these sites and applications have risen from mere technological tool to magical power towards mass decision making. Hundreds of thousands of internet users are so conditioned to using social media. My study explores the influence of social media from the rural marginalized, who are poor and illiterate, have little or no access to education, skill training and other means of social mobility. Such a phenomenon is very rampant especially in the underdeveloped countries, and there is an ever-widening gap between the standards of living of young people in the economically developed and developing countries (Encyclopedia.uia.org, 2020). Memes have been extensively used as a source of communication and news since the last two decades. The use of it in various fields has been an upsurge in recent times. The influence of contents shared through political memes over the internet and its impact on a youth"s perception, ideologies, and decision making are the concern. Humour and satire involved in the memes are the key influencing factors for making political decisions. They create a safe ground for ideologies and propaganda in simple contextual depictions. There could be a whole lot of idea which the youth prefer; factual or appealing data and in what ways do political meme creators use this to their benefit. (Syed Saad, 2021). Such affiliation could even reflect in their choice of voting pattern in the electoral politics.

◦ Background of the Study

Social media networking being the ever-present and powerful component of todays" communication industry, even the mainstream political parties do not want to ignore the use of it. They want to make it part and parcel of their political agenda to be set and to be achieved. These communication components are made to believe that they determine and control the very voting behavior of people at large. Thus the compulsive social media discourses and habits of the users are adapted in commercial marketing success, policy making, political campaign and electoral success. In the internet revolution, society experiences a new way to interact. Social Media is the buzz medium which is a fusion of society, technological growth, new media innovation, transformation in communication. Millions of people use social media for communication, sharing information, collaboration, entertainment and placement seeing and many more. A total of 5.07 billion people around the world use internet today - equivalent to 63.5 percent of the world's total population. (MilinduTissera, 2021). Internet users continue to increase with the latest data indicating that the world"s connected population grew by more than 170 million in the last 12 months till October 2022. Internet users continue to increase at an annual rate of 3.5 percent and current trends suggest that two-thirds of the world"s population should be online by the end of 2023. Social media use continues to grow and the global user total reaching 4.75 billion in October 2022. That is equal to 59.3 percent of all the people on Earth. It indicates that more than 93 percent of people are internet users. The number of social media users around the world has increased by just over 4 percent in the past 12 months. 190 million new users have joined social media between October 2021 to October 2022. It equates to growth of more than half a million new users every day. It means that social media users are currently growing at a rate of 6 new users every single second (datareportal.com- global threat report, 2022).World Internet Usage and Population Statistics 2022 estimates that the Asian population makes the

54.9 percent of the world population. The penetration rate i.e. internet users in 2022 is 67.4 percent. This makes the 53.6 percent of the world total internet users (internetworldstats.com, 2022).

Aim and Objective

Youth being the maximum users of social media networking, the aim for the study is to discover the framework of social media contents namely WhatsApp memes as motivators in political campaigns on rural youth. WhatsApp political memes might influence them as

one of the path-breaking tools towards their political image making. The objectives of this study are,

- To assess the impact of political memes on youth as an instrument of influence in their political engagements and decisions.
- To explore the effectiveness of political memes as a medium for persuasive communication.

My work experience and involvement with rural youth for a decade has led me to study the impact of this mechanism towards their civic and political engagement.

Review of Literature

The importance of social media is a tool for citizens to craft alternative narratives which are sometimes in stark opposition to mainstream media coverage (Maggie Dwyer and Thomas Molony - 2019). The participatory nature of online media activism facilitates translation of information into action. The use of social networking by the youth promotes in themselves civic involvement and political engagement towards self-identification as a citizen. It develops collective sensibility. It makes the youth politically active by way of collective finding, sharing, discussing and mobilizing themselves around political issues (Ellen Middaugh, Lynn Schofield Clark and Parissa J. Ballard (2017). The extensive use of Social Networking in India has been on the rise among the new generation youths. In today"s world, life cannot be imagined without Facebook, YouTube, Instagram, WhatsApp, LinkedIn or Twitter accounts and online handles. The new age social networking culture has been well accepted and has met an enthusiastic response and acceptance. Exploration on some online surveys shows that there is an aaccidental exposure to politics on social media in three major European countries such as Germany, Italy, and the United Kingdom. The assessment has shown that the accidental exposure to political information on social media contributes to citizens" online political participation in comparative perspective. Social media networking may appear to be thin modality of civic engagement which might not lead to conventionally impactful action but they do enable gestures that carry symbolic weight for individuals, typically by giving voice and affording visibility to issues generally marginalized *(Papacharissi, 2015)*. Memes have been proven to be great persuasive means for generating images and opinions into the minds of civilians. They can be used for propaganda to reinforce ideologies, identities and stereotypes. It has also been noted that during the World War One, memes were used in the form of satirical texts, image and artistic expression. Even in such times poets and artists were hired to create comics and awareness messages in posters and newspapers (Leong, 2015). The dynamism of internet trends is bombarded by the „Meme Culture". The flexibility of moulding a meme into a device of humour, cultural resonance, representative of identities along with a sense of soft comfort enables us to investigate it as an appropriation of cyber culture for localized political means with high possibility for socializing citizens to strive for becoming „Critical status quo as part of a more extensive network of political action" (Shobha Vadrevu, 2013).

Methodology

It is basically a quantitative study for which I have taken 112 samples of rural and marginalised youth. Their views, concepts, opinions and experiences on the effects of political memes are analysed. Literature was explored in ResearchGate, Academia, Scopus, Google scholar, Orca online and Research Cardiff with the key words "social media", "politics", political affiliation, "political campaign" and rural youth for the period starting from 2015 till 2022. The keywords were restricted to search only the titles, abstracts and author specified keywords provided in the research and conference papers. Some information about research during these years is evaluated by this literature survey. The selected areas are provided by these platforms the combination of quality and quantity of research papers sourced from the topics of social sciences and humanities. These sections identify the trends in research publication in the context of usage of social media for political purposes. The study paper is done from quantitative research type making use of question and answers from hundred and twelve samples. These are from college going rural youth mainly from Thiruvannamalai district and a few neighbouring districts of the similar social stratum - rural and marginalised. The sample selection and technique are as follow. The Procedure was, for data collection, marginalized youths from a few districts were approached. The purpose and nature of this quantitative study was explained to them. They were also informed that their participation is voluntary, and they may choose not to participate. The structured questionnaire with ten questions was used to register their responses. The construction of questionnaire is that the research tool consists of ten questions excluding the given demographic profile of the hundred and twelve respondents - college going rural youth. Questions are developed based on the probable impact of social media on their intellectual level, emotional level, interest level, recreational level and aspiration level. The construction of the questionnaire is attached in the appendices.

Analysis of the Data

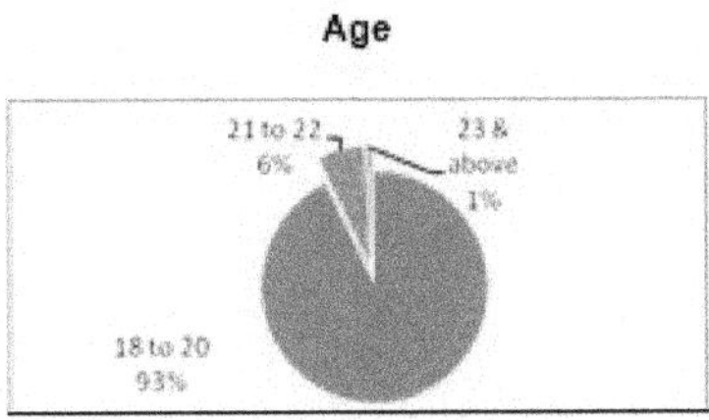

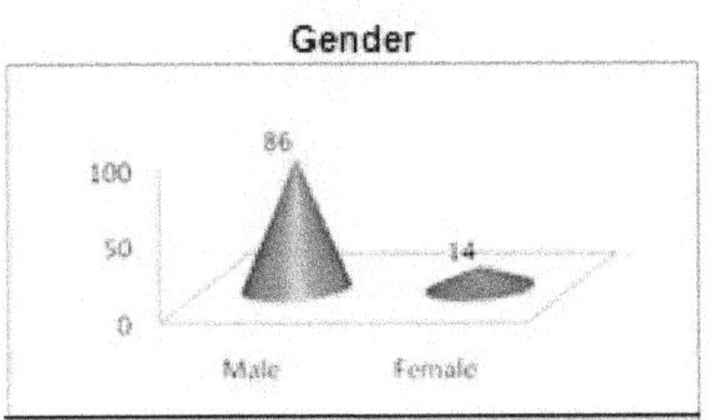

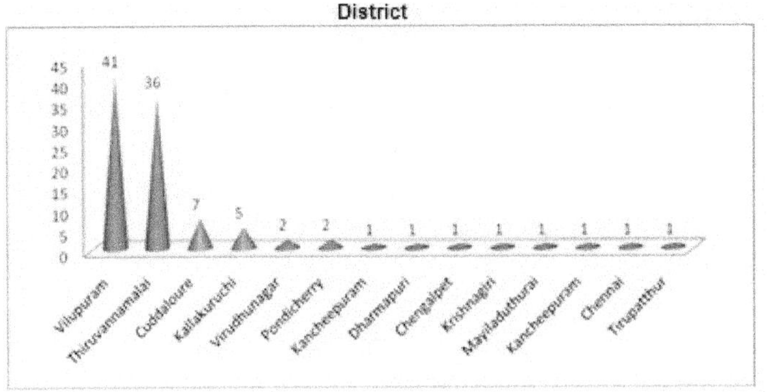

In percentages

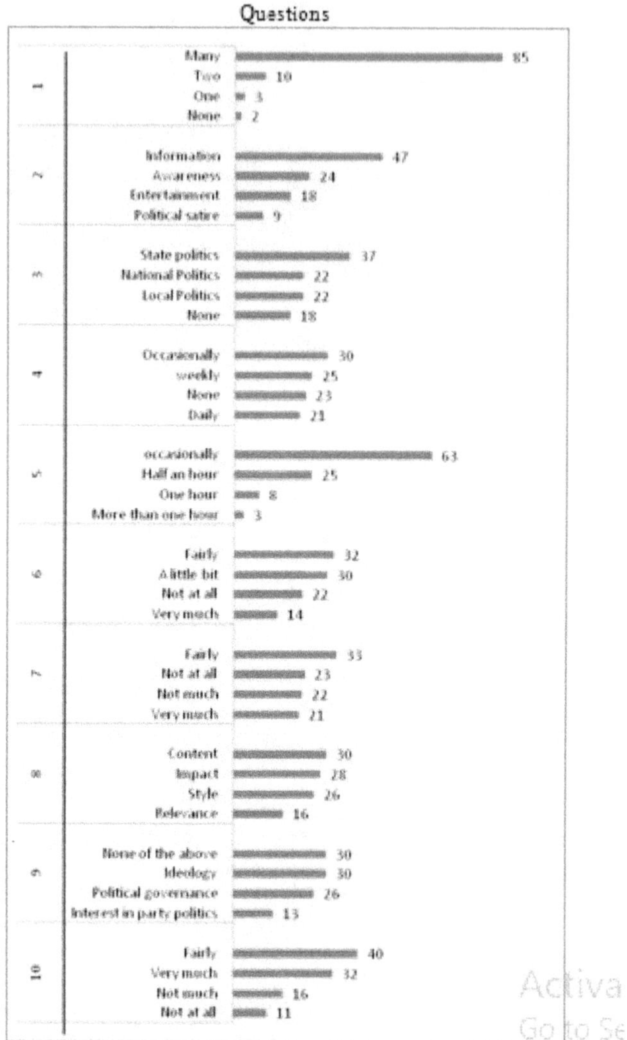

Anova

Test of difference

Age vs. Overall memes attitude

Hypothesis: There is no significant difference between the age groups towards the overall memes attitude

		Sum of Squares	df	Mean Square	F	Sig.
Age	Between Groups	2.474	22	0.112	1.269	0.215
	Within Groups	7.796	88	0.089		
	Total	10.270	110			

Table 1

Since the P value (0.215) is more than 0.050, the null hypothesis is accepted and concluded that no significant difference is established between the age groups.

Anova

Test of difference Districts vs. Overall memes attitude

Hypothesis: There is no significant difference between the districts towards the overall

memes attitude

		Sum of Squares	df	Mean Square	F	Sig.
Gender	Between Groups	3.863	22	0.176	1.572	0.042
	Within Groups	9.831	88	0.112		
	Total	13.694	110			

Table 2

Since the P value (0.835) is more than 0.050, the null hypothesis is accepted and concluded that no significant difference is established between the districts.

Overall Memes Attitude

	Frequency	Percent
Low	31	28
Average	60	54
High	20	18
Total	111	100.0

Attitude * Gender Cross tabulation				
Count				
		Gender		Total
		Male	Female	
Attitude	Low	27	4	31
	Average	54	6	60
	High	15	5	20
Total		96	15	111

Enter Caption

Findings and Recommendations

After analyzing the response acquired from the online questionnaire sampling, the summary of it indicates that these rural youths generally engage themselves in political memes as source of news dissemination in proportion to the percentage of data analyzed. The humour and satirical mode of conveyance are appealing to them and even the covered up harsh reality is much easily imparted smoothly in proportion to the percentage of data analyzed. The quantitative test shows that the overall levels of political memes consumption and political interest are proportionately moderate. The range of involvement in political affiliation moderately broadens in proportion to the data obtained.

The ANOVAs Test of difference shows that in the age and overall memes attitude, there is no significant difference between them. Since the probability of obtaining value is more, the null hypothesis is accepted and concluded that no significant difference is established between the age groups. The test of difference in gender and overall memes attitude shows that there is no significant difference between them. Since the probability of obtaining value is less, the null hypothesis is rejected and concluded that 5% level (average) significant difference is established between the gender groups. The test of difference in districts versus overall memes attitude shows that there is no significant difference between the districts towards the overall memes attitude. The probability of obtaining value is more; so the null hypothesis is accepted and concluded that no significant difference is established between /among districts.

The primary data required for the study have been drawn directly from the college going students through structured questionnaire. The secondary source of information is collected mostly from internet sources and conference paper and journals. Stratified random sampling technique was applied. The data gathered from the students was quantitative in nature with the help of coding technique in the SPSS Anova.

Further Scope of Research

The brief literature review points to the focus area of research that could investigate the use of social media for political affiliation of youth in general and rural youth in particular. Future research may utilize the categorization of youth in rural areas in Tamil Nadu based on their political affiliation, political interest and social media use with particular reference to whatsapp political memes: as politically critical youth; politically disengaged youth. The further study may help to explain the influence and behavior of social media better in the context of rural youth in Tamil Nadu.

References

1. https://www.internetworldstats.com/stats.htm#:~:text=WORLD%20INTERNET%20USA GE,0.6%20%25, 2022.

2. https://datareportal.com/global-digital-overview-Global Threat Report, 2022.

3. Milindu Tissera - In-Depth Analysis of the Most Significant Cybersecurity Events and Trends of 2021, 2021.

4. https://www.researchgate.net/profile/Syed-Saad-7, 2021.

5. http://encyclopedia.uia.org/en/problem/138877, 2020

6. https://www.tandfonline.com/doi/full/10.1080/ 25729861.2021.1973291, 2019.

7. Maggie Dwyer and Thomas Molony, 2019.

8. https://www.researchgate.net/profile/Ellen-Middaugh-2, 2017.

9. Ellen Middaugh, Lynn Schofield Clark and Parissa J. Ballard, 2017.

10. Papacharissi,https://www.researchgate.net/journal/Social-Media-Society-2056-3051, 2015.

11. Leong, https://zfin.org/ZDB-PUB-160107-6#, 2015.

12. https://www.goodreads.com/author/show/4548988.R_J_Parker, 2014. 13.https://www.igi-global.com/chapter/the-use-of-twitter-during-the-2013-protests-in- brazil/238224, 2013.

13. Shobha Vadrevu, https://www.researchgate.net/profile/Shobha-Vadrevu, 2013.

14. https://www.researchgate.net/profile/Karin-Becker, 2004.

CHAPTER FIVE

Thematic Analysis of Social Stigma of Transgender People in Global Newspapers Using Media Frames

Kirthana S.P[1], Department of Communication and Media studies, Bharathiar University, spkirthana112@gmail.com

Dr. M. Srihari[2], Department of Communication and Media studies, Bharathiar University, shbharathiar@gmail.com

Abstract

The sex and sexual identity social norms by the media have the power to influence public perception, especially attitudes toward transsexuality. Many transgender persons come out in the world in an effort to promote gender diversity in all countries. The gay community in India establishes the shared objective of enlightening people on important transphobia and inclusion concerns. They deal with regressive things like oppression, brutality, injustice, and prejudice. The media has a significant impact on how transgender persons are portrayed since it reflects how society views them and how societal stigma changes as awareness grows. This study uses media frames to examine issues of societal stigma of transgender individuals in major international newspapers (Times of India and USA Today). This study's objective is to analyze the published articles' content in light of framing patterns connected to deviance, abnormality, religion, victimhood, and equal rights to ensure that their representation reaches a wider audience. Additionally, it seeks to comprehend and compare the themes of societal stigma against violence, discrimination, and transphobia in newspaper stories. Mass media contact theory emphasizes that media operates as an extension of real-life contact to get key information sources about transgender people. The intercoder reliability is calculated for each variable and implications of intrinsic stories as a source of mass-mediated contact to promote gender visibility of trans people are discussed.

Keywords: Transgender people, Media framing, Transphobia, Social Stigma, Violence, Discrimination, Mass media contact theory

Introduction and Review of Literature

Transgender is an umbrella term used to represent gender variant people whose lifestyles conflict with the gender norms in society (Whittle et al., 2007). According to The Transgender Persons (Protection of Rights) Act, 2019, the term transgender people is, 'a person whose gender does not match with the gender assigned to that person at birth including trans man or trans woman irrespective of Sex Reassignment Surgery or hormone therapy, person with intersex variations, gender queer and person having socio-cultural identities like hijras, enunchs, kothis, jogappas, aravanis, kinnars etc'.

Prevailing norms of binary gender construction in most societies, the representation of transgender people and gender diversity has increased in recent years (Gates, 2011). Hall (1997) contends that representation, in general, is the use of language "to say something meaningful about, or to represent, the world meaningfully to other people".

Pertaining to one's gender, gender roles in society are assigned that an individual is expected to act and conduct according to their assigned sex (Satish Chandra, 2021). This shows how people are socialized to understand and enact gender (Christian N. Thoroughgood et al., 2020).

Their basic tenets of equality to choose their gender to which they belongs to is intrinsic to the 'right of choice and self-determination' (Tewari, Upadhyay and Singh (2020). Their choice of gender transition in the socially constructed bifold gender society made them naïve to social stigma associated with discrimination, violence and transphobia.

Social Stigma

Transgender people are usually seen as social deviants (India Exclusion Report 2013-14; Jama Shelton et al., 2017) as they chose their preferred gender over biological sex assigned at birth. Also, they are stigmatized and targeted for discrimination. Ryan and Futternman (1997) has found in his study that they are generally more stigmatized than LGB community in contemporary society and need more support and services. According to

Goffman (1963), 'stigma implies devaluation and rejection, and connects the marked person with socially devalued or undesirable characteristics'. The discrimination and prejudice stigmatisation (Satish Chandra, 2017) refers to enacted stigma ((Pescosolido & Martin, 2015) that includes rejection, exclusion, verbal abuse, bullying and physical violence (Budge, Adelson, et al., 2013; Budge, Katz-Wise, et al., 2013; Februari, 2013; Keuzenkamp, 2012; Kuyper, 2012; Miller & Grollman, 2015; Norton & Herek, 2013; Stotzer, 2009).

As new schemes and programs are coming up benefitting transgender people in India, their acceptance in society is still abstruse (Kuyper, 2016). Stigma against transgender people refers to devaluing gender non-conforming people and developing negative attitudes towards them (Ministry Of Social Justice And Empowerment, 2014). It includes discrimination, violence, exclusion in the public sphere, transphobia that lowers the level of tolerance towards them.

Discrimination and Violence

According to the report submitted by the Ministry Of Social Justice And Empowerment, 2014, discrimination states that "an action that treats people unfairly because of their membership in a particular social group". Transgender people face discrimination, violence and mistreated in every walks of life (Revathi, 2010; Vivek Diwan et al., 2016; Ramos, 2018; TOI, 2022) from subtle to severe (Bazargn and galvan, 2012, Chung and brack, 2012). They are treated indignified and with inequality surviving under extreme hostile contexts (Vivek Diwan et al., 2016). Burgees and Mallon (1999) stated that they face discrimination in school, housing, health care constraining them to live outside the mainstream society. Discrimination includes, assuming a person with their birth sex and not using person's preferred name or pronoun, asking inappropriate question about their bodies, refusing access to housing, or extreme acts of violence (American psychologist, 2015) and generalised attitude of looking upon them as sex solicitors (Satish chandra, 2017).

Discrimination and Violence in Family

Transgender people, at the time of gender transition experience familial violence (Vivek Divan et a. 2016), as most families cannot accept the gender non-conforming behavior in their children (Satish Chandra, 2017; Chakrapani et.al. 2010; Leelavathy, 2014). Krug et al (2002) describes violence as "the intentional use of physical force or power, threatened or actual, against oneself, another person, or against a group or community, that either result in or has a high likelihood of resulting in injury, death, psychological harm, mal development, or deprivation".

A study related to this consummated that very few show their willingness to support their loved ones without trying to make them change. (Chakrapani, V. &Dhall, P. (2011). Evident in India Exclusion Report 2013-14 by Shubha Chacko and Arvind Narrain and a transgender author Revathi, 2010 publicly claims to prevent transgender people from transition, the family adopt forceful methods like administering electric shock to genitals, forcing to take male harmone tablets, marriage compulsion (Sheena Rajan Philip, 2018) believing that it will arouse a man inside them. Many researchers demonstrated family rejection and in condition to mute their identity (India Exclusion Report 2013-14) they are accepted within the family. Many researchers found that one's dissatisfaction with birth sex can lead to loneliness and other psychological problems (Dhejne et al., 2016; Februari,2013; Keuzenkamp,2012; Keuzenkamp & Kuyper, 2013; Testa et al., 2017).

Having discriminated by their own family members (India Exclusion Report 2013-14), they flee from the house seeking gender acceptance, experiencing homelessness (Anton B S, 2009; Shelton, 2015). This ostracism within families often continues across the lifespan of transgender people. Identically, the violence extends to the neighbourhood, peers experiencing verbal, physical, and sexual abuse. (Chakrapani, V. &Dhall, P. (2011). Grosssman (2006) observed that without these support, they often drop out of school, run away and end on streets engaging survival sex at risk of STI.

Discrimination at public sphere

In terms of social exclusion in the public sphere, Priya & Kumar (2021) discerned that transgender people in the public sphere are pushed towards the margins of society due to their gender non-conformity, resulting in stigma, violence, humiliation, torture, and exclusion.

Vindicating this concept, Habermas (1989) inferred "the legal inclusion of transgender people does not translate into social acceptance due to the heteronormative and exclusionary nature of the public sphere". Public space is central in the formation of public and public culture (Amin(2005)), the heterosexual norms of the public sphere cause discrimination against the third gender in the public space (Satish Chandra, 2017). Each group appearing in the public claims and uses the public space according to its socially prescribed roles (Weisman, 1994). But when transgender people show their gender visibility in public space, they became victims of discrimination and violence (Budge et al., 2013; Corrigan et al., 2013; India Exclusion Report 2013-14; Miller & Grollman, 2015) and even sexual assault (India Exclusion Report 2013-14). Maris et al., (2020) noticed that due to the visibility of their third gender, they report forms of enacted stigma lie stared at, laughed at, abused and avoidance. He also interpreted that there is higher frequency of enacted stigmatisation experiences after transition of trans women. Misgendering by voice is another problem raised due to their gender identity as Pasricha et al. (2008) found in their study about communicative satisfaction among trans women. Due to the gender visibility, they face unwanted attention, harassment and discrimination in public space and accessing public services (India Exclusion Report 2013-14).

School, being the basic public space that everyone intends to share with others, due to prejudice discrimination (Jama Shelton et al., 2017; Sheena Rajan Philip, 2018) and bullying at school many discontinue their studies (Vivek Divan et al, 2016; American psychologist, 2015; Singh and Jackson, 2012; Satish Chandra, 2017), few advancing to higher education (Berkins, 2007). According to UNESCO, 2012 reports that 50% of gender non-conforming children dropout from school due to bullying in India. Revathi (2010) a transgender found that a school is one of the most violent spaces for children who do not behave according to heterosexual conventions.

Trans people are mostly unemployed (Anton B S, 2009) and if employed, they are discriminated widely in workplace (Sheena Rajan Philip, 2018) at most all phases of recruitment (Suriyasarn, 2017; Brewster et al, 2014) and devaluation (Bockting et al. 2013). Grant et al., 2011 found that there is significant relationship between discrimination at workplace leading to survival sex or selling drugs. The act of discrimination has extension even in providing health care to trans people. The National transgender discrimination survey, 2011 reported that 19% transgender were refused care due to discrimination and 50% reported that they had to educate the health care providers about transgender non-conforming care.

Regarding their discrimination over gender identity transgender people face violence. The transgender people has been a victim to brutal physical assault by vigilante elements ((Ramos, 2018)) of society (India Exclusion Report 2013-14). Along with beatings, they were threatened and sexually harassed like feeling their breasts, stripping them and even raping them (India Exclusion Report 2013-14).

Transphobia

Redman (2018) found in his study that transexuality in all its forms is associated with prejudice and misunderstanding. Prejudice is defined as 'negative attitudes about an outgroup, is a root cause of numerous adverse social, political, and health outcomes' (Broockman and Kalla, 2016). He also postulated that prejudicial thoughts could produce lasting changes in attitudes toward an outgroup. Semmalar (2017) argues that the disempowerment of the trans community in India is the result of many factors, transphobia is one among them. Personal contact or knowing someone who is a transgender is positively associated with positive attitude towards them (Tadlock et al., 2017), reducing transphobia. Sheena Rajan Philip (2018) in her study observed that 40 % of the cis people reported that they have fear to interact with transgender and 82% possess has a predefined notion that transpeople will convert their gender too. It is also found that 78 % believed that their existence is a threat to the society.

Casey (2016) approached in the study showing that disgust reactions towards transgender people affect their attitude towards them. Flores, 2015 in his study demonstrated that transphobia puts transgender people upto 25 times greater risk of abuse, assault and suicide. Driven by a desire to punish the people who defy from existing gender norms, gender based violence attacks are performed (UN high commissioner for human rights (2011) and the transphobia surrounds them fuels violence against them. (Vivek Divan et al., 2016). Transphobic violence such as physical assault or psychological violence (Revathi, 2010) has been recorded in all parts of the world (India Exclusion Report 2013-14).

Significance of Media Framing

Media plays an important role in representation and proliferation of transgender people in recent years. They are pivotal in defining what is normal, acceptable or desirable (Fleras, 2014) "Media is one discourse that reflects and creates reality, working within a complex tapestry of discourses to create and recreate cultural understandings" (Mocarski, Butler, Holt, Huit, Hope, Meyer, & Woodruff (2019). Media as a key information source effectively reach out to more people, has the potential to set social norms regarding sexual identity, as such shape public opinion (Calzo & Ward, 2009; Lee & Hicks, 2011; Sink & Mastro, 2017; Markel et al, 2017).

While media visibility is seen as a key vehicle for their political emancipation and a precondition for the recognition of their rights and legitimacy as a social group (Jacobs & Meeusen (2020)), media representation can affect how people evaluate trans people. Media representation can create larger awareness about the culture of transgender in real-time contact. Nabi and Oliver (2009) opine that media representation connotes public impression of a person including their gender, 'media depictions of deviant behaviour are influential, they imply, not necessarily because they directly convince people that certain behaviours are immoral'.

Mass mediated exposure operates as a catalyst in aiding knowledge to the individuals about LGBT people who lack direct contact with their culture. The assumption was endorsed by the mass media contact theory. It states that contact with individual group members, under particular circumstances (pertaining to the nature and quality of the contact and the context in which it occurs), operates as a catalyst for tolerance toward that group (Jacobs & Meeusen (2020)). Media contact with trans people increase empathy and decrease bias (Hoffarth and Hodson, 2018), thus the exposure effects decreasing transsphobia, increases support for the transgender rights (Flores et al., 2018)

Hardy(2014) stated that mainstream publications with their larger readerships can exercise their position of power to eradicate injustice. Larger readership publications create larger awareness about the culture of transgender in real-time contact pertinent to framing. As well as the media frames can contribute to the semantic memories the public has about the transgender population (Matthews (2016)). Media practices facilitates discussion among the public about the oppressed and their need for social acceptance. Their framing of news stories can reflect public opinion and so Journos place themselves in the position of power.

During the early years, news stories facilitated perspectives regarding homosexuality as an immoral, mental abnormality, contemporary narratives are embracing them as a legitimate group in the society struggling for recognition and acceptance. This is mainly after the annulment of 377 of IPC in the year 2017, that the trans community gained visibility in pop culture. This way of media framing can affect political agenda-setting and can initiate policy making changes regarding transgender issues (Li, 2017).

Khalil, Lakho, Bari, Soomro (2020) from their study state that the representation of transgender community is underrepresented and is a challenge to the social construction of gender (S. Kessler and W. Mekenna (1978). Besides underrepresentation, they were marginalised and their activities were banned to maintain social order (Reddy, 2006).

Representing them socially in media can enhance social support and constructive stigmas related to them. Furthermore, it mainstreams the third gender into the normative binary gender existing in society.

Framing refers to the way information is packaged in the news (De Vreese, 2005). Frames can organize messages, adds interpretation to the issues. In a national survey it is found that one third of the people use media whether online or other news media as a primary source of information about transgender issues (Taylor, Lewis, and Haider-Markel, 2018).

News often portrays transgenders as different from deviant sexual behaviour, with immoral and criminal urges, given their marginalized position in the society earlier (Adamczyk, Kim, & Schmuhl, 2017; Baisley, 2015). The deviance frame draws transgender as a fundamental threat to the social order, focusing on unsafe sex, HIV/AIDS, criminal behaviour (Jacobs & Meeusen, 2020).

Abnormality framing of transgender frames gender transistion as a mental disorder and an abnormal lifestyle (Alwood, 1996; Hart, 2000). "This abnormality frame stresses contrasts between heterosexuality and homosexuality, clarifying that while homosexuality may be tolerated, it is by no means natural" states Vanlee et al., 2018.

In some stories, transsexuality is placed in a religious context with leading religions accepting or condemning homosexual behaviour building religious belief systems (Adamczyk et al., 2017). Stone (2019) finds that representing transgender women as dangerous strangers were common.

The equal rights frame stresses transgender as third enders who constantly fight for their respect, equal opportunities (Baisley, 2015; Moscowitz, 2010) boosting tolerance and acceptance. Framing of their rights issues in media is the need to create familiarity to the public (Tadloc, 2014). Another recurring narrative frame depicting transgenders as victims of discrimination, mental abuse, physical violence and sexual harassment (Warren & Bloch, 2014). The study discusses all the five frames in text with transgender content stories published in global newspapers.

Rationale of the study

In the bi-fold gender society where homosexuality is still associated with prejudice and misunderstandings (Redman, 2018), the consciousness towards their emotional struggles, inclusion, spectrum and sexuality was held high in India (India Today, 2019). It is also obvious that many disclose their gender identity ahead of existing social norms. So it becomes expedient to understand the social stigma associated with transgender people and their framing in global newspaper.

Objectives

The objective of the study is,

- To analyse the content of published articles using media framing patters of deviance, abnormality, religion, victimhood, and equal rights
- To examine the themes of societal stigma against violence, discrimination, and transphobia in newspaper stories.

Research Questions

Based on the objective, the research questions formulated are,

- What are the most used framing patterns of the published content in the newspaper?
- Does the subject analysis of newspaper has significant representation of transgender related stories?
- Does themes published in newspaper stress significant importance in bringing out the social stigma of violence, discrimination and transphobia that transgender people suffer from?
- How is the portrayal of the social stigma against transgender people in global newspaper?

Research Methodoloy

The study focuses on transgender related stories published in two international newspapers (Times of India and USA Today), which has the largest readership globally available online between the timeline March, 2022 to August 31, 2022 (post pandemic period). Based on the previous research (Alwood, 1996; Moscowitz, 2010) mentioned by Jacobs (2020), five frames were coded: deviance, abnormality, religion, victimization, and equal rights.

a. The deviance frame depicts transgender people as a threat to social order focusing on unsafe sex, criminal behaviour and promiscuity.
b. Abnormality frame stresses homosexuality as a mental disorder and abnormal living.
c. Religious frame argues homosexuality on the religious grounds of traditional belief systems.

d. Victimizing frame portrays transgender as victims of discrimination and physical, mental and sexual abuse.

e. Equal rights frame is the emerging frame that values trans people as a social group with legitimate demand of respect, human rights ensuring equal opportunities.

This resulted in 58 stories between the time lapses that represented transgender issues that are central to the narrative. All 55 stories (24 from Times of India and 31 from USA Today) were subsequently coded using a pre-tested coding scheme. Inter-coder reliability was assessed for all the 55 stories and Krippendorff's coefficient of 0.81, it is customary to require alpha greater than 0.8.

Analysis and Findings:

Each story taken for analyses will have different frames. The central narrative of the story is considered for particular frames. The figure 1 and figure 2 analyse the subject of the stories placed in the particular newspaper TOI and USA Today respectively. Most of the stories were categorized under world stories (42%) in TOI and Sports Stories (43%) in USA Today. It reveals that the stories related to transgender reach global audience and the frames that these news stories carry has greater significance in portrayal and acceptance of them in mainstream society.

Most of the stories in this subject matter contain a positive tone and emphasized equal rights frame supporting the struggles of trans persons in society. It brings out their emotions, respect they needed in society, equal opportunities they demand, rights of the transgender community, pride march organized by them ensuring recognition. Entertainment restrain stories that interest the public including cinema portrayal, theatre plays performed by transgenders, business news, book reviews related to transgenders etc.

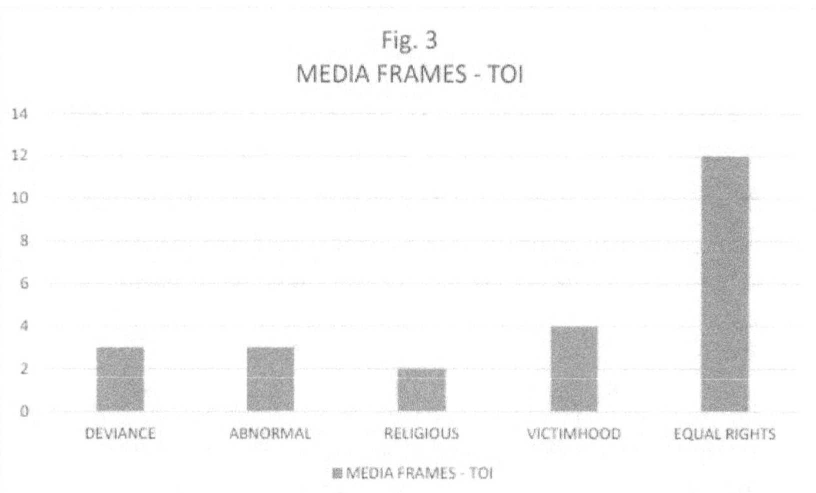

Figure 3 plots the frames of articles published in 'Times of India' newspaper. The frequently used frame in India Today is the equal rights frame, followed by the victimization frame. Expressed in an article that the parents of transgender children are ready to accept their relationship at times on condition of not expressing their gender out of closet. The parents should understand their struggles instead and accept them within family. It comments about the right to be within their own family and ways the community tries to part them out of the society. There exists transphobia because of lack of information and awareness about their gender identity was asserted. Talking about discrimination that transgender face is not obvious. It takes forms of physical, social, institutional. A statement, "A transgender person is someone who the doctors made a mistake about when they were born," "But some people, when they get a little bit older, realize what the doctor said was not right", expressed transgender as abnormal person framing abnormality in media.

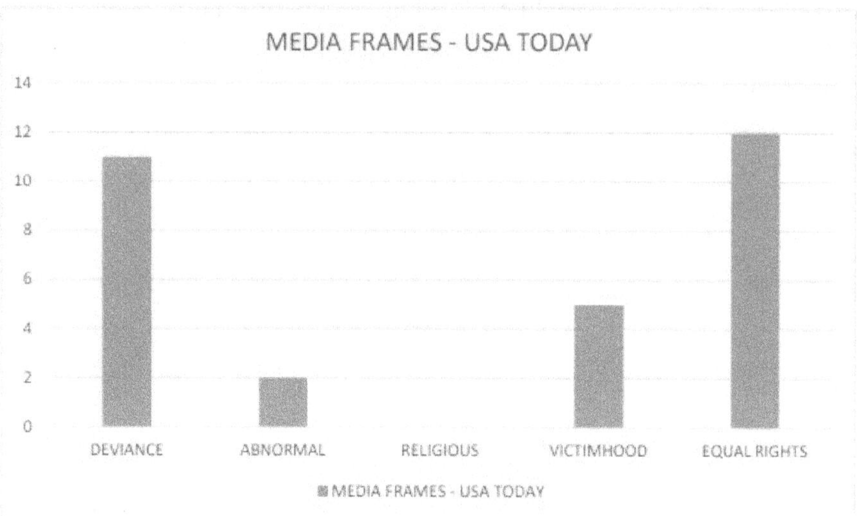

Similarly, Figure **4** graphs the frames in USA Today as the equal rights frame followed by the deviance frame and victimisation frame. The statement "Just changing your parts doesn't make you a woman" exihibits deviance frame. There are stories related to ascertain the activities done to a transgender kid preventing gender transition was right, indicates abnormality and deviance framing. Everyone has a right to feel comfortable with their bodies and live their own life. 'I transitioned to be happy, to be true to myself" said Transgender swimmer Lia Thomas expressing her right to live happy in the world without one's validation to their gender. Youth are seeing themselves reflected in the media and on the internet, so they are less afraid of exploring and acting upon being trans or gender diverse, it concedes.

Integrating the media frames, it is clear that there is an increasing use of equal rights frames than all other frames in newspapers taken for analysis. It entails that the use of equal rights frame in most of the news stories related to transgender people, it express the support for gender identity that their existence normalizing the third gender improving education and employment opportunities. This again in turn will enhance their livelihood and societal acceptance. The representation of the victim frame is followed greatly after the equal rights frame where transgenders are depicted as victims of discrimination, physical violence, mental abuse about their gender, sexual harassment etc. Victim framing stories discuss the discrimination they face at school, sports, hospital, government office, accessing health care services, getting legal documents with recognition to their gender, denial of public services, physical, mental and sexual violence by their family members, friends, relatives and others.

The immoral and deviant behavioural depiction ascribed to transgenders like unsafe sexual contact and promiscuity, carrier of AIDS/HIV, allusions to the pervasive nature of homosexuality, crime, pedophilia on deviance frame holds considerable representation compared to others as there is more discussion about the ban of third gender in international sports evens. Moreover, abnormality frame compassing narratives underscoring homosexuality as a mental disease or an abnormality is also undersized.

Consummately, the depiction of transgender in equal right frames, the media visibility on transgender community have grown positively in shaping the public opinion about homosexuality. This boost tolerance towards third gender groups providing equal rights and opportunities for respectful livelihood. Representing transgenders in an equal rights frame will create positive public opinion about them to heterogeneous groups present globally thus denouncing the acts of discrimination and abuse against them from prejudice and stereotypical portrayal in other media as well. Similarly, the overt expressions of prejudice have been discredited, suggesting that deviance and abnormality frames will be less acceptable (Herek & McLemore, 2013). The secularization is resulting in a shift in news coverage among journalists in the frames of equal rights than on deviance and abnormality. Media representation in an equal rights frame will contribute to a positive opinion about their gender identity in popular culture, internalizing transgender identity as normal. The effect of positive exposure creates attention to mass-mediated people about transgender people coinciding with a wave of tolerance and accepting them in the phase of normalization, busting the myth of binary gender construction. It also acts as a vehicle of intergroup contact and reduces prejudice.

Conclusion

Most relevant in establishing harmony with nature among the prevalence of fluid gender identities is media. Media practices result in media frames (Matthews (2016)). It facilitates discussion among the public about the oppressed and their need for social acceptance. Their framing of news stories can reflect public opinion and so Journos place themselves in the position of power. In the study it is analyzed, the consciousness related to transgender about emotional struggles, inclusion, spectrum and sexuality was held high (India Today, 2019). Many younger individuals come out recognising transgender as a result of growing acceptance and improved media representation (USA Today, 2022). Media can be a powerful tool in shaping opinion about sexual minorities especially transgender because it acts as a catalyst along the same line of real-life intergroup contact theory (Calzo & Ward, 2009; Sink & Mastro,2017). Media framing can affect political agenda-setting and can initiate policy making changes regarding transgender issues (Li, 2017). Moreover, portraying them in the equal rights frame creates awareness for the equal treatment of transgender people in society and equal opportunities in the education and employment sectors.

The portrayal of LGBT people should meet some criteria regarding the nature of this contact in order to boost tolerance (Ortiz & Harwood, 2007; Riggle et al., 1996; Sink & Mastro, 2017). The study interprets that the depiction of transgender-related stories is significantly high in the frames of equal rights than other frames of victimization and religion. This is a step forward towards the gender emancipation of the trans community.

New frames on journalists shift from problematizing homosexuality and transsexuality to problematizing homophobia and transphobia have emerged (Jacobs & Meeusen (2020)). This shift will operate as an impetus in shaping the minds of the public and tolerance towards transgender people. Media interventions can alter the attitude of common public towards gender diversity. As Media has power to reach larger audience, media frames are important to create impact (India Exclusion Report 2013-14).

Correlating the results of this study, Austin and Goodman (2017) found that there is positive sift in social attitudes towards trans individuals because of media attention. Personal contact or knowing someone who is a transgender is positively associated with positive attitude towards them (Tadlock et al., 2017), reducing transphobia. This can be perceived as advantageous as research by Bariola et al. (2015) suggests that frequent contact with transgender peers was associated with greater resilience

Future research can elaborate on assessing the active representation, tone of articles combining news and public opinion data on other mediums as well as other frames.

References

Alwood, E. (1996). Straight news: Gay men, lesbians and the news media. New York, NY: Columbia University Press.

Association, A. P. (2015). Guidelines for psychological practices with transgender and gender non conforming people. American Psychologist.

Calzo, J. P., & Ward, M. L. (2009). *Media exposure and viewers' attitudes toward homosexuality: Evidence for mainstreaming or resonance?* Journal of Broadcasting & Electronic Media, 53(2), 280–299.

Chandra, S. (2017). Transgender children education and their reengagement in Society.

David Brookman, J. K. (2021). *Durably reducing transphobia: A field experiment on door to door cancvassing.* sciencemag.

Engel, S. M. (2013). Frame spillover: *Media framing and public opinion of a multifaceted LGBT rights agenda. Law and Social Inquiry,* 38(2), 403–441

Fleras, A. (2014). The media gaze: Representations of diversities in Canada. Vancouver,BC: University of British Columbia Press.

Gates G. J. (2011). How many people are lesbian, gay, bisexual, and transgender. Los Angeles, CA: The Williams Institute.

Hall, S. (Ed.). (1997). Representation: Cultural representations and signifying practices. London, UK: Sage.

Hardy, J. (2014). Critical political economy of the media: An introduction. Oxford: Routledge.

Laura Jacobs & Cecil Meeusen (2020) *Coming Out of the Closet, Also on the News? A Longitudinal Content Analysis of Patterns in Visibility, Tone and Framing of LGBTs on Television News (1986-2017),* Journal of Homosexuality.

Matthews, T. R., (2016). *Decolonizing transness in sport media:The frames and depictions of Transgender athletes in Sports illustrated.* Colorado, Colorado State University.

Mocarski, R., King, R., Butler, S., Holt, N. R., Huit, T. Z., Hope, D. A., Meyer, H. M., & Woodruff, N. (2019). *The Rise of Transgender and Gender Diverse Representation in the Media: Impacts on the Population.* Communication, culture & critique, 12(3), 416–433.

Nabi, R. L., & Oliver, M. B. (2009). The Sage handbook of media processes and effects. Sage.

Narrain, S. (2018, September 16). Love after the time of 377. India Today.   https://www.indiatoday.in/magazine/cover-story/story/20180924-love-after-the-time-of- 3771338619-2018-09-15

O. (2018, September 15). No more are we invisible. India Today. https://www.indiatoday.in/magazine/cover-story/story/20180924-no-more-are-we- invisible1338621-2018-09-15

Ramos, R. c. (2018). The voice of an Indian transwoman: A hijra autobiography.

Redman, S. M. (2018). *Effects of same-sex legislation on attitudes toward homosexuality.*

Political Research Quarterly, 71, 628–641.

Shubha Chacko, A. N. (2013-2014). India Inclusion Report.

Tewari, A., Upadhyay, S., Singh, V., (2020). *Transgender rights, the 'Third Gender' and transforming the workplace in India.*

Tuchman, G. (1978). *Introduction: The symbolic annihilation of women by the mass media.* In

G. Tuchman, A. K. Daniels, & J. Benet (Eds.), Heart and home: Images of women in the mass media (pp. 3–38). New York: Oxford University Press.

Vivek Divan, C. C. (2016). *Transgender social inclusion and equality: a pivotal path to development.* Journal of International AIDS Society.

India's Soft Power Diplomacy towards Southeast Asia

LalhmingSangi
Research Scholar, Department of Political Science
Mizoram University
Dr. JC Zomuanthanga
Assistant Professor,Department of Political Science
Mizoram University

Abstract

India is often referred to as an example of soft power because of its historical legacy and modern values on the international stage. India is a growing economy with the potential to grow significantly and is also a multicultural democracy with a generally positive foreign influence.The expansion of soft power in India has taken many different shapes under successive governments. The people of India and Southeast Asian countries have shared common traits in terms of culture and trade. Even during the colonial period, both India and Southeast Asia shared a common feeling of brotherhood in their struggles against imperialism. In this regard, India's cooperation with Southeast Asian countries has become an important phenomenon on both sides. This paper examinesthe idea of soft power as a crucial component of India's foreign policy in the twenty-first century. Secondly, it also focuses on India's soft power strategies with Southeast Asian nations. Lastly, it also analysesIndia's interaction with ASEAN concerning cultural diplomacy since the post-independence period.

Keywords: *Soft Power, Culture, Southeast Asia, Foreign Policy*

Introduction

In the truest form, we live in a global village now. Everything has been simpler, better, and smooth as a result of globalisation, free markets, and geopolitics, whether it is the enormously open worldwide markets or quick communication. Today, no nation can exist on its own without considering the international consequences of even the smallest of its actions. Foreign policy and bilateral relations are now an essential part of international diplomacy.Joseph Nye was the first person to introduce the concept of soft power. He classified such diplomacy according to its fundamental sources, which are political principles, international affairs, and culture.India is a progressive nation with a strong soft power heritage. The nation is acutely aware of the importance of its cultural engagement and has to exert a bit more effort to make its culture fascinating to the rest of the world.

Meaning of Soft Power

A simple definition of soft power diplomacy is the ability to make an influence that ultimately resulted in the desired outcome without the use of coercive power, wealth, or strength.It is simply the use of alternative resources such as values and traditions to form the opinions of others, either by attempting to make them connect to the same perspective to attain cohesively set goals.India's constantly expanding population may be a blessing in disguise since one of the benefits of our diversity specifically, our cultural diversity is that it benefits us.The Indian subcontinent is made up of a variety of customs and heritages that blend harmoniously into the overall image because some rulers built their bases there over the years.

The expression "soft power" may be understood in terms of a usable national capacity to advance foreign policy objectives and priorities of a country by non-coercive means. Being an ability to shape a broader narrative in bilateral and multilateral diplomacy, it remains a vital instrument in foreign policy by itself or as a complement to the application of "hard power", that is, military power or other types of compelling diplomacy. As a culturally diverse, democratic country with a large aspirational, extroversive population pursuing socio-economic mobility, India's image is that of a benign country confident of its growing role in the international community in support of democracy, international cooperation, stability, and commitment to multilateralism as an effective way to meet our common global challenges.

Soft Power in India's Foreign Policy

A country cannot pick its neighbours. Thus, neighbourhood policy becomes essential for any country. Typically, interactions and disputes with neighbours are more pronounced. The mindsets, perspectives, and visions of nations are influenced by history. It is clear that while soft power may be a prerequisite for success, it is not adequate in and of itself. This is so because decisions made on foreign policy are not made unilaterally.Some of the connections with other entities are also established by them. A nation develops its capabilities through time.These can be in the realms of technology, business, or the military. A nation's foreign policy strategies change when new capabilities are developed. Capabilities become important in the context of "Soft Power". How can your interests be safeguarded? What instruments do you employ? These inquiries have been made by strategic thinkers throughout history. In his Arthashastra, our own Kautilya discusses the four Upayas, or instruments to be used, as well as the six stratagems, or Shadgunyas. Saam, Dhaan, Bhed, and Dhand are these. The first two of these preferences are for peaceful methods and rewards.

India envisions a peaceful, liberal, largely pluralistic, and non-violent world order with non-threatening global leadership. Luminaries like Mahatma Gandhi and Rabindranath Tagore, as well as the arts of literature, music, dance, the software sector, Ayurveda, etc., create a staggering variety of soft power assets that promote India's appeal to the world's population. Indians are known for their core values of respect, harmony, and brotherhood, with Ashoka, Buddha, and Gandhi serving as the main examples. The famous Greek works Odyssey and Iliad are contrasted with mythological epics like the Mahabharata and Ramayana. Between 1 and 1000 AD, India's GDP, which was also higher than China at the time, earned it the nickname "Golden Bird". Eventually, this led to the arrival in India of emigrants, traders, and invaders like "Alexander the Great".

Jews, Christians, Muslims, and members of several other faiths have all been given protection and freedom of religion in India over the years. India's history and culture, which she has left to the world, show the evolution of her past and how she peacefully accepted other religions without losing sight of her own culture and history. The foundation of India's international image is the concept of "unity in diversity" which is reflective of the diverse range of cultures and civilizations that continue to captivate people around the world. The rootlets of soft power spread far. Indian soft power is praised for fostering positive relationships with other countries through tradition, religion, ethno-linguistics, and language. The outside world found everything about Indian culture to be fascinating. In addition to "soft" power, India committed itself to advance internationally through trade and statecraft. The concept of "VasudhaivaKutumbakam" was introduced to the world and to India through the Upanishads. Chanakya, a renowned ancient Indian philosopher used grants and non-aggression agreements to acquire control over neighbouring nations, which highlights the importance of soft power in ancient Indian statecraft.

The use of culture in foreign relations is significant for several factors. Human interaction via culture establishes the foundation for long-lasting relationships through the respect that is instilled in people. Thus, this humanistic basis establishes a solid platform for subsequent accords. Since the beginning, Indian culture has been gaining traction on the international stage. Our cultural legacy has helped our booming reputation stand out; whether it is because of the attention we received as one of the oldest civilizations in the world, the different foods, or yoga. It wouldn't be completely wrong to say that Prime Minister NarendraModi has shifted the aim of using soft power as a means to objectively build India's relations across the world and make our foreign policies and relations much stronger. This has improved India's standing as a viable nation with the ability to flourish both politically and economically, in addition to assisting India in achieving its foreign policy goals. It also demonstrates our capacity and readiness to play a significant role in international strategy.

India is becoming more self-assured in presenting both its historical history and its modern principles on a global scale, which is excellent news for the world order, which is in desperate need of role models. The best defence against authoritarianism and the spread of extremism around the world is a diverse democracy that is financially prosperous. India is variously referred to as a model of soft power because it is the largest democracy in the world and also the country with the greatest number of impoverished people. For some, India's rich culture and democracy stand in contrast to other authoritarian and revisionist great powers, and many Indian leaders do speak favourably about the country's potential for soft power.

Even after the end of the Cold War, India's soft power appeal was still evident. The Association of Southeast Asian Nations (ASEAN), which recognised the appeal of India's expanding economy and democratic ideals, integrated India into Asian institutions during the 1990's. In its interactions with the rest of the world, India has discovered that soft power is an essential but insufficient component. It has frequently reaped genuine, material benefits from its soft power as a democracy with a vibrant culture and some aspect of morality in its international participation. To better communicate its culture and principles to audiences around the world, it has work to do.

India and Southeast Asia

The development of cultural and religious dissemination of Hinduism, Buddhism and Islam mainly spread to Southeast Asia from India and this impact went moderately through China by the land and maritime way. Though India had little knowledge about its neighbours in the initial years culturally it has had a deep connection with them since the seventh century. Thus, religious propagation and cultural linkages have raised the relations between India and Southeast Asia to a higher stage when India is actively conscious of the federation of Asia for peaceful coordination to all to abstain from British supremacy.

Most importantly, the history of India and Southeast Asian countries has been intertwined through a political discourse but primarily through ideas, knowledge, traditions, civilizational elements and commerce traversing among these countries on the high seas of the Indian Ocean, Malacca Straits and maritime exchanges. It underlines that the history of such relations between India and ASEAN is based on the history of civilizational and cultural exchanges as the strong foundation for relationships in the contemporary period. Culture has acquired a new prominence in the present times. It has been variously described as soft power leading to cultural diplomacy. Culture does play the role of a strong bridge of understanding and friendship amongst different societies. Culture has also played the role of soft power to lubricate the process of interstate dialogue by attracting others rather than creating a threat. Hollywood and Bollywood are perhaps the two best examples of such soft power instruments throughout the world. In this regard, Indian Bollywood actors are a household name in Southeast Asia. Most interestingly, the joint India-ASEAN cultural performance brought out the common traditions of performing arts which have evolved between India and these countries in their distinct manner with a strong connection over a millennium of history.

The rising of ASEAN by the late 1980's has given opportunities for other states to play a larger role in their activities. India being strategically close to the heart of ASEAN members has fortunately changed their long-lost chances of becoming a dialogue partner which has been initiated since the birth of ASEAN thus the key unsettling issue between Singapore and India began eroding paving more way for a balanced approach.The end of the Cold War has carried India as well as Southeast Asia more closely. India has been looking towards the East since ancient times and it is widely evident that India and the East have shared connection and the spread of Indian cultural inspirations leads to the enrichment of Southeast Asian countries have shown the fruitful link between India and the East. So, Indian customs, traditions and its Hindu rituals were not new to Southeast Asian countries and these brought unity and a feeling of oneness between India and Southeast Asian countries.

The Look East Policy's (LEP) active use of cultural diplomacy has made it easier to recognise efforts toward the sincere appreciation of these nations rather than being seen as an endeavour to establish cultural supremacy over them. One instance of this is the ASEAN-India Free Trade Area (AIFTA).The availability of power resources affects the efficacy of both hard and soft power strategies.The Modi administration's effort to use soft power is intended to position New Delhi at a crucial time while most of the world still views India as a relatively tolerant and multicultural democracy with a largely benign international influence as well as an emerging economy with the potential to become a significant economic success story. The cultural ties between India and East, Southeast, the Middle East, and Central Asia highlight India's long history as a melting pot of different religions and cultures. Hinduism travelled to Southeast Asia, Islam connected India to Central Asia, and Buddhism spread from India to China and beyond.

India's relations with ASEAN members unfolded since the launching of LEP. Thus, the wave of LEP had a good impact on the Southeast Asian region. The neglect of cooperation has been revived and there was a drastic change in India's economic relations with ASEAN members. PM Vajpayee has reactivated interest and he visited several Southeast Asian countries in 2000, 2001, 2002 and 2003. These visits were reciprocated during the same period by various dignitaries from Southeast Asia. India's relations with ASEAN grow significantly after she became a Full Dialogue Partner and its relations with Singapore formed the first priority as it is the most powerful partner of India from the perception of bilateral economic cooperation while India has good relations with other ASEAN member like Myanmar with its cultural and religious belief. The key principles and objectives of "Act East Policy" are to promote economic cooperation, cultural ties and to develop a strategic relationship with countries in the Asia-Pacific region.

The industrial development of India was the best guarantee for the economic recovery of Southeast Asia mainly because the economies of

India and Southeast Asia were complementary and not competitive, and the greatest cooperation between the two is necessary for the good of all. This led to increased exchanges; other geopolitical developments soon grabbed hold of the global agenda. Likewise, foreign direct investment has also boomed with ASEAN-5 (Indonesia, Malaysia, the Philippines, Singapore and Thailand).

India's rich and ancient past has produced a number of academicians, thinkers, and researchers who have dedicated themselves to the formation of unique schools of knowledge, a pearl of wisdom that has travelled and established itself well beyond the boundaries of India. The most notable hubs of cultural synthesis and soft power were India's historic institutions, which attracted many academics and students from around the globe.Academicians, intellectuals, and people from a variety of sectors have been drawn to India because of its mystic civilisation, which has also sparked the interest of many Indologists. The global market, notably in Asia, West Asia, Europe, and Africa, is more broadly impacted by Indian society and culture, which includes Indian cuisines, religions, festivals, spirituality, yoga, movies, and music.The Incredible India tourism campaign played a crucial part in establishing "Brand India", the term used to characterise the initiative launched by India to generate interest and position India as a suitable target for investment. India could be counted among the countries with strong soft power potential. People from all over the world are attracted to the nation because of its vibrant democracy, an independent judiciary, role for NGOs, and progressive and independent media.

India's soft power has developed into the capacity to forge new relationships, fortify existing ones, and mend rifts caused by political and historical events. India promoted peaceful development, a good neighbourly policy, and the use of soft power in the 1990s to bolster its foreign policy and strengthen its standing in South Asia.India's soft power, which has been dispersed throughout her broad social and cultural legacy for millennia, demonstrates her commitment to secularism, liberalism, and inclusion of all cultures—goals that are more crucial in today's restless society. One such aspect of Indian soft power around the world is the experience of South-South cooperation and enduring solidarity with poor countries. Gandhian nonviolence principles, Nehru's Five Postulates of Panchsheel (Peaceful Coexistence), and the widely backed Non-Aligned Movement (NAM) during the Cold War made the NAM a major player in international associations.

India's rechristened AEP further strengthened India's connection with Southeast Asia and pushed India in strengthening relations through greater cultural and economic exchanges. Thus, the Comprehensive Economic Cooperation signed between India and ASEAN further improved the economic cooperation as this eliminated tariff barriers among all the members and establish free trade in goods, services and investment. India and ASEAN relations have been growing and along with this India's relations with Singapore have also increased as Singapore's export and import items have played a powerful role in India and ASEAN growing relations. India and ASEAN are a future prospect in the Asia-Pacific region and India's AEP became an important apparatus for India in engaging with the East Asian countries through economic and communication technology.

Jawaharlal Nehru, India's first Prime Minister, received the assurance that his nation was committed to playing a significant and helpful role in international affairs. India has a reputation for fostering dialogue, culture, and cooperation in the advancement of world politics. His Holiness the Dalai Lama, the spiritual head of the Tibetan people, said that 'the rich legacy of religious tolerance in India can serve as a model for the entire world'. The economic liberalisation and globalisation that have taken place have enhanced the interdependence of the many countries in the world. Today, soft power is seen as the key component of a country's overall power. It has the power to strengthen a community's commitment and resolve and provide a country more control over its international affairs. Additionally, soft power has developed into a key tool for deciding India's foreign policy and strategic choices.

Conclusion

Soft power has the potential to enhance India's reputation and carve out a place for the nation in the current global order because physical force cannot be used outside of a frontier or territory. The perception that India in the present period is considerably more robust than it was several decades ago has been established by the symbols of soft power as well as other advancements.The enormous magnetism that the Indian diaspora possesses in the living nations where they reside can significantly contribute to the expansion of the soft power of the nation.

To restore its national image, India must identify its strengths. India's ages-old knowledge and spirituality ought to persuade other countries to recognise its potential for global leadership.India, although having abundant soft power resources, does not have an institutional framework to harness soft power and advance its national interests abroad. Due to significant issues including corruption, poverty, violence against women, antagonism against commerce, pollution in metropolitan areas, caste prejudice, and gender inequality, India has performed poorly in the categories of national appeal.

References

Amstrong, Shiro and Tom Westland.(2018).Asian Economic Integration in an Era of Global Uncertainty. Australia: Anu Press

Basu, Dr.Koyel. (2017). India-ASEAN Relations in the 21st Century: Exploration of the China Factor. Global Journal Of Human-Social Science. Vol. 17.Issue 5

Blank, Jonah, Jennifer D.P. Moroney, Angel Rabasa, Bonny Lin. (2015).Look East, Cross Black Waters: India's Interest in Southeast Asia.United States: Rand Corporation

Chaudary, Dipanjan Roy. (September, 2017). India gains from soft power in South East Asia. The Economic Times

Cheok, Cheong Kee and Yong Chen Chen. (2019). Assessing ASEAN's Relevance: Have the Right Questions Been Asked? Journal of Southeast Asian Economies

Grare, Frederic and Amitabh Mattoo. (2001). India and ASEAN The Politics of India's Look East Policy. New Delhi: Manohar Publishers

Jaishankar, Dhruva. (September, 2018). India rising: Soft Power and the world's largest democracy. Brookings

Mazumdar, Kumar Asis. (1982). South-East Asia In Indian Foreign Policy: A Study Of India's Relations With South-East Asian Countries From 1962-82. Calcutta: NayoPrakash Publication

Muni, SD andRahul Mishra. (2019). India's Eastward Engagement From Antiquity to Act East Policy. New Delhi: Sage Publications India

Outlook.(July, 2022).Soft Power Central To Rebalancing World Order, Working Naturally To India's Advantage: EAM Jaishankar

Ram, Amar Nath. (2015). India's Asia-Pacific Engagement Impulses And Imperatives. New Delhi: Manohar Publishers

Reddy, K. Raja. (ed). (2005). India and ASEAN Foreign Policy Dimensions for the 21st Century. New Delhi: New Century Publications

Severino, Rodolfo C. (2008). ASEAN Southeast Asia Background Series No. 10. Singapore: ISEAS

Viswanathan, H.H.S. (September, 2019). India's Soft Power Diplomacy.Ministry of External Affairs.

Yahya, Faizal. (2003). India and Southeast Asia: Revisited. Contemporary Southeast Asia.Vol. 25.No. 1. pp. 79-100

• 70 •

New Media, Changing Rituals, and Impact on Married Couples with Special Reference to Assamese Weddings

Ms. Farha Yashmin Rohman
Ph.D. Research Scholar
The Assam Royal Global University
Email: farhayasminrohman@gmail.com
Ms. Anindita Dey
Ph.D. Research Scholar
The Assam Royal Global University
Email: anin0812@gmail.com

Abstract

Our daily lives have been significantly impacted by modern technology, particularly new media. There are both positive and negative repercussions, and because we are digitally dependent, we are more open and conscious of a variety of events that have been occurring in our life for some time. Various cultural rituals are observed by new media consumers related to marriages, and some of these rituals have been significantly followed while others have been completely eliminated. Cultural hegemony of various cultures is being upgraded and flourished in the minds of couples by various new media handles, thereby altering society's attitude towards wedding rituals. With regard to Assamese weddings, how sangeet ceremonies have been added, and how bride and grooms are under immense pressure to organise sangeet ceremonies by looking at their friends' images that have been uploaded to their various social media accounts. Various couples have also been seen undertaking pre-wedding shootings and hire professional videographers / photographers for which they chose specific venues, which are later uploaded in various digital platforms. Bachelorette party is also seen as a ritual these days. Couples nowadays commonly create a hashtag shortly after being engaged, and hashtags are frequently used to capture the entire process. This is done to keep their friends, family, and visitors informed if they are unable to attend the wedding. This study will explore how new media and specially Facebook is influencing the rituals of a marriage and how married couples, or the would-be couples are under pressurised because of the new media for following or not following various wedding rituals. To study the changing rituals because of Facebook, a survey will be conducted followed by help taken from the primary and secondary sources. The study aims to investigate how couples are personalizing their wedding rituals and doing away with old customs. As a whole, the paper will focus on the elements that influence new media and altering rituals, as well as their impact on married couples.

Keywords:New media, Married couples, Rituals, Hegemony, Assamese Weddings.

Introduction

A wedding is one of the auspicious rituals that many cultures of the world consistently share. A ritual that is found in almost every single society. Leslie Baxter and Dawn O. Bracewaite explain that marriage is a ritual A voluntary, structured and cultural norm-based communication event that pays homage. What is considered sacred to create and recreate the identity of a couple or family. Weddings are patterned in the sense that most ceremonies have models or a wide range of scripts follow. Weddings are guided by cultural norms. In short, culture influences wedding expectations. The ritual and the marriage of the couple continue. That means they worship something sacred A wedding is a collection of relationships, families, religions, marriages, and more. Social system. Weddings include the identities of individuals and newlyweds. Weddings are not something a couple can do alone-they are sociable in nature. Weddings normally take place in the context of social interactions within a network of relationships.

Wedding Rituals

When we talk about weddings in India, weddings in India are more than just rituals. Hindu weddings in India are more than just ceremonies. It is a luxury celebration and a beautiful union of the two souls. Marriage is a gathering of two families, celebrating an eternal bond. Hindu weddings are so colourful that they are attracting the attention of people all over the world. Hindu weddings, usually characterized by their magnificent features, feature multi-page invitations, numerous guests, and a luxurious feast. Each Hindu wedding ceremony symbolizes something unique, and each ritual has a meaning behind it. Even at Saatpheras (Seven rounds), each round proposes a vow to be taken by the bride and groom. The ritual is so elaborate that Hindu weddings usually last until 3 AM. With dances at sangeet and baraat, stunningly beautiful mandap, elaborate robes, mehendi, haldi, juta chhupaai till the emotional vidaai, Hindu weddings are a powerful and emotional sight. In addition to the rituals that take place on the day of the wedding, there are many other rituals that are part of a Hindu wedding that takes place a few days before the actual wedding.

New Media, Changing Rituals and Impact on Married Couples

The impact of social media is widespread. It has changed the way people spend their vacation. It has changed the way we look for jobs. Marriage plans have also changed over the years. There are significant differences between today's ideal wedding as well as the ideal wedding of the pre-social era. Obviously, wedding costs were affected as well. Now it's not difficult to understand the role that social media plays. Prior to social media, wedding planning was done on weekends and after work. The couple flipped through magazines, visited places to wear black ties and dresses, went to sample caterers, explored potential venues, and planned their reception when they weren't busy with anything else. Wedding plans were waiting when they were busy with other things. I can't wait for my wedding plan anymore. Now it's a phone. Bride and groom can keep browser tabs open on Instagram and Pinterest pages full of wedding ideas. The wedding planner can be accessed from the messaging app. All of this makes it very easy to add another element to your wedding or reception to make it "perfect."

Endless rituals, elaborate rituals, hundreds and even thousands of guests. Weddings in India are world-famous for their luxury, and greater than the celebration of life. However, over time, the basic structure of Indian weddings has undergone a paradigm shift. But today, newlyweds are ready to share their wedding day not only with their loved ones but with others around the world. Social media plays an active role here. Social media is pressing us to show only the best of our lives. This effort for perfection also affects our mental health. We do our best only when it comes to relationships, careers, vacations, weddings and honeymoons. Looking up is an unrealistic ideal, as the bride and groom do not see the shortcomings or frustrations of others. There is pressure to find the perfect cake, book the perfect venue, and agree to the biggest reception explosion as the ring continues. Couples often struggle to choose the ideal hashtag to promote their wedding. There is also the DIY(Do it Yourself) pressure of sites like Pinterest, where one can choose the perfect flowers, decorations, and spreads. Snapchat only offers wedding filters. With constant exposure and pressure, the stress of it all can be very real and detrimental to the couple.

In a country known for luxury and bigger weddings , social media plays a supporting role in perfecting D-day without complications. There was a time when brides were just flipping through magazines, watching film scenes, shows looking for ideas that would lead to their dream wedding, but social media is now taking up that space. The bride puts too much pressure on herself to pin the perfect outfit on Pinterest and share d day photos on Instagram and Facebook. Social media enhances the wedding planning process, making it much easier to find and discover brands, venues, make-up artists, hair stylists, wedding dress designers, asking brides, brides 'mothers, grooms' mothers. I'm applying pressure. Perfect for their wedding day. Currently, there are more than 20 reality TV wedding shows that focus on how wedding planners create elaborate weddings and how brides decide to find the perfect wedding dress. Shows like "Say Yes to The Dress", Bridezillas, Band Baajaa and Bride. According to an article in The Free Press Journal where the ace Indian Fashion Designer stated that because of Exposure to global trends in social media it manages to put real pressure on those hosting weddings. Bride and groom, and close relatives who feel this increasing pressure to compete in a particular way.

With the advent of the new media, it plays a significant role in our everyday lives, especially when it comes to weddings, which are celebrated in a grand manner in this country. People feel the pressure to create a 'picture perfect' D-day because they have become more dependent on digital technology. There is no shortage of wedding trends to explore when planning. From creative dessert spreads to elaborate photo booths, modern weddings are full of fun breaks from tradition. A hype is created as soon as the couple announces that they are engaged and one of these new trends is wedding hashtags. Many couples are advised to use custom wedding hashtags when posting to social media during celebrations, as guests want to share your big day. Hashtags are usually a pun or creative twist on a couple's name. Every social media account displays hashtags along with photos, videos, and reels. The hashtags are also used in the wedding invitations as well. In fact, a separate Facebook account or page is now created in order to post visuals related to their wedding. Due to such shows and various designers taking their designers to Instagram and blogs it becomes difficult for the designers. Creating something special for brides who are exposed to world trends and "The first thing a girl (bride) says is that she wants something different. It's safe to say that social media has had the greatest impact on weddings, but it's important to understand that what's posted online isn't something you see every time, and it's people who create social trends.

Several Insta pages and websites are currently promoting newlyweds, grooms, and men's disturbers, which are displayed in a successful way to convince brides and grooms to give gifts to their cousins and friends. These gifts are customized according to the couple's demand. Bridesmaid gifts are a way to thank you for being part of your wedding. Similarly, guest are also given customized gifts, messages along with sweets to the guest who were part of couple's special day.

Wedding photos aren't just about poses and smiles. Unlike before, photographers have come up with innovative ways to perfect a wedding album. If you want to take a pre-wedding photo a couple of months before your wedding, you need to know the photographer in advance. So you can be completely relaxed in front of the camera and be yourself. It can help your photographer discover your best angle and position to make your wedding day photo stand out. In addition, pre-wedding photography can be considered a rehearsal photography session to prepare for a big day. Pre wedding shoots are now also seen in the assamese weddings as well were couples hire professionals. This is often endorsed by the famous songs sung by Assam's industry singers or songs from Hindi Cinema.

There is also a ceremony known as "Kalire Ceremony" which are often seen amongst the North Indians, but now even other communities also follow this ritual. The ceremony often takes place ahead of the wedding. Those who attend a Christian wedding may feel déjà vu at the moment of Kalire Ceremony. They will undoubtedly associate the scene with the tradition of throwing bridesmaids (and brothers) among bridesmaids and blessing them with the bliss of marriage. Here the bride turns and throws a bouquet at the designated enthusiastic junta. The lucky one with the bouquet has some of the bride's luck and is believed to be in the next line to get married. Many ceremonies, often shared on digital media from accounts, often hold the hearts of couples trying to get married. They try to create new trends and share them across different platforms, including some rituals that were not previously part of the wedding.

Over the years the cost of the weddings have risen drastically , each and every ceremonies are celebrated larger than life . Events like Sangeet almost always have a Bollywood atmosphere, awards ceremonies, and can be seen at Assam's wedding. Earlier women folk would sit together and sing using traditional musical instruments , now along with that sangeet function is organised and only ladies were allowed to attend. Nowadays participants are no longer restricted . Sangeet today is celebrated by both bride and groom's family together in a common place. The performance is held on a big stage. The choreographer teaches cool dance moves throughout the procession of relatives. Relatives occur in pairs or groups. Generally, the bride and groom's parents have a set. Some of them even hire DJs to create an atmosphere where guests can dance to their heart's content. Some hire musicians, while actors perform at their ceremonies.

According to an article in Vogue written by Nupur Saryaiya, where Kainaz Sethna, co-founder of Mumbai-based firm Seven Step had stated that how a popular platform Instagram has changed the way we record the most important moments of our lives. So it is no coincidence that the role of social media platforms in wedding planning has also changed. Nearly a billion Instagram users include tons of inspiring wedding photos, custom wedding hashtags. She also stated that this platform is a double-edged sword. New media has also influenced creative concepts and experiences, including minimalist yet surreal decor, Instagram-worthy fusion dishes, and the virtual presence of the entire wedding through. trailers, movies and documentaries, among other things. The path used to influence can be a major source of unnecessary stress and pressure to throw a perfect celebration. Many couples getting married today have been exposed to marital assaults on social media for more than a decade. Not only does this create a sense of pressure to have a grand wedding, but it also gives them time to dream big. Social media has made weddings more glamorous. Social media directly impacts the overall cost and luxury of these special events. And as more and more "generation of social networks" grow, this trend will only increase.

Study Gap

Research has been done on how the new media has managed to instil dread of luxury among various couples who are getting married or are already married, and ever since they began to incorporate ceremonies and rituals that were previously not included. When it comes to the presence of digital media, platforms like Facebook have played a significant influence. Such medium can occasionally influence a couple's wedding-day decisions and even have an impact on the entire wedding process. The medium has also played a significant part in influencing people to follow a perfect picturesque and popular wedding. As a result, it is critical to understand the elements that encourage couples to follow the trends that are being discussed on social media. Therefore, it has been observed that no research has been done on how new media and ceremonial changes and its impact on the couples, especially in the context of weddings in Assam. Hence, the researcher in this study tries to observe the impact of social media specially the Facebook on married couples and their take on changing rituals because of the new medi

Research Question

- Is the Facebook changing the wedding rituals in Assamese weddings?
- How are the married couples impacted by Facebook posts on rituals related to weddings?
- What are the factors influencing the change in Assamese weddings?
- Are couples under pressure to adopt to new trends of rituals because of Facebook?

Research Objective

- Understanding how new media is changing Assamese weddings trends
- To study if Facebook posts are influencing couples adopt new rituals during weddings
- To analyze the factors influencing changes in Assamese weddings.
- To understand if couples are pressurized to perform certain rituals during weddings which was not Important before.

Review of Literature

"How Indian weddings have evolved in the last decade" written by Nupur Saryaiya . It had noted how digital media had been able to influence and put undue pressure on the couple to organize a picture-perfect party. This on article " *Shaadi Squad tells us why social media is important for wedding planning in 2019"* written by LathaSunadhmentioned how trending hashtags to boomerangs to drone shots, social media is now a huge driver of marriages. Which are helping creating virtual memories by expressing real emotions is the age of Instagram stories and Facebook videos. The author also stated that In today's digital age, couples have a burning desire to share this important milestone in their relationships with others. This can come in the form of an Instagram Live or Facebook post and is often very sentimental. Moreover, this trend has captured all Indians, from the wealthy to the middle class. Nowadays Wedding photographers and filmmakers are now well thought out and carefully selected mostly by seeing their previous works. Earlier All wedding albums looked exactly the same, surrounded by cliché poses and boring shots. Those images could not capture the essence. The strangeness of tradition, the moment of an intimate groom, the honest enjoyment and much more. Also today's couples want to document everything and proudly share it on their social media profiles. That's probably why wedding coverage has evolved so much. Includes teaser, trailer, and finally a wedding movie. And of course, beautiful pre-wedding photo shoots in exotic locations and jointly agreed hashtags to help you find event posts on social media. In an article written by Andrew Arnold titled *"How Social Media Has Transformed The Idea And Costs Of The Ideal Wedding"*Before social media, wedding planning was done on weekends or after work. The couple browsed several articles, film scenes, couples visiting places to pick up a suit and dresses, checking out available locations and planning decorations accordingly, and seeking appointments during off-peak hours or when the couple is free from their respective work. Earlier one had to wait for the plans to be excited but now everything is done over the phone. The bride and groom can open a browser tab to Instagram and Pinterest pages full of wedding ideas or follow pages specifically made for wedding occasions. The wedding / event planner are available through the messaging applications which are available on their websites along with their several social media handles. All of this makes it much easier to add one more element to your wedding or reception to make it "perfect". Recently an article in Outlook titled *"The Emerging Trend Of Planning Weddings Digitally With Shaadi Wish"* .Created by Anvir Shergill

and Divyata Shergill, ShaadiWish is India's most daring online wedding planning portal, strategically helping future couples and families plan their weddings online and wedding agencies create a digital marketplace for work. Thanks to the reliability and hard work of digital wedding planning platforms like ShaadiWish, potential couples can plan their wedding at the push of a button.

Methodology

To complete the study , the researcher here sought help using both primary and secondary methods. The main method used was survey method. The method here not only helped to collect required data but also to complete the investigation. The survey was created in google form for an easy distribution online. These were Facebook, Instagram , WhatsApp, Gmail and Messenger. Robson (2002) defines it as: —The theoretical, political and philosophical background of social research and its impact on research practices and use of specific research methods. According to Morvaridi (2005)The main methods of social science and humanities are research methodologies quantitative and qualitative research. Researchers have gathered 100 samples of those who have been married forabout five years. The respondents participating in this study residing will be from Guwahati, Assam. This study helped to find out how the married people faced the pressure to include certain rituals which were newly added just to be part of the on-going social trends. The goal of the study is to find out how couples are personalising their wedding ceremonies and abandoning old traditions. The study will concentrate on the factors that influence newmedia and changing rituals, as well as their impact on married couples as a whole.

Data Analysis

The survey was conducted in Guwahati based on the opinions of 100 married people. Out of these, 39% are 26-30, 27% are 18-25, 19% are 31-35, and the remaining 15% are 36- 40-year-old profession including lawyers, professors, research scientists, engineers, graphic designers, doctors, housewives, entrepreneurs, chefs, optometrists, fashion designers and journalists as shown below

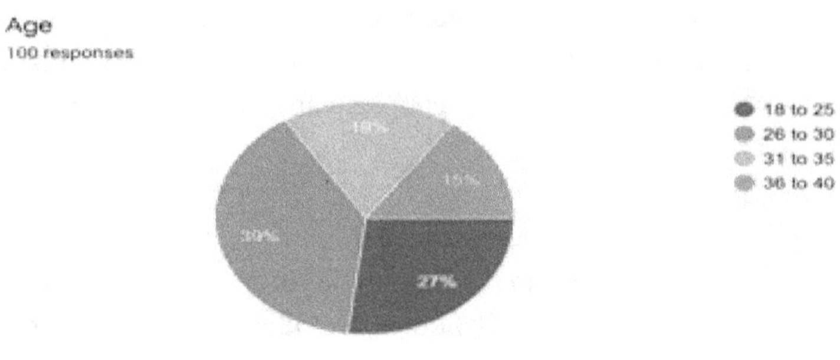

Fig 1

As shown in fig. 2, it has been found that out of the 100 respondents, 67% were women and 33% were men. All respondents are married. Out of the 100 respondents, 42% have been married for less than a year, 31% for 4-5 years, 21% for 1-2 years, and the remaining 5% and 1% in 2-3 years and 3-4 years, respectively

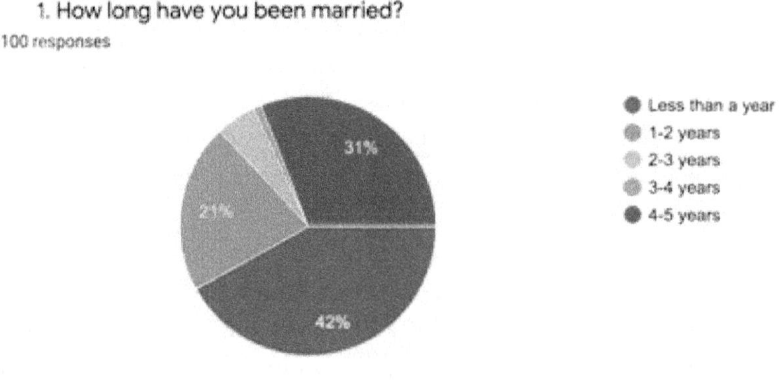

Fig 2

As shown in fig. 2, it has been found that out of the 100 respondents, 67% were women and 33% were men. All respondents are married. Out of the 100 respondents, 42% have been married for less than a year, 31% for

4-5 years, 21% for 1-2 years, and the remaining 5% and 1% in 2-3 years and 3-4 years, respectively.

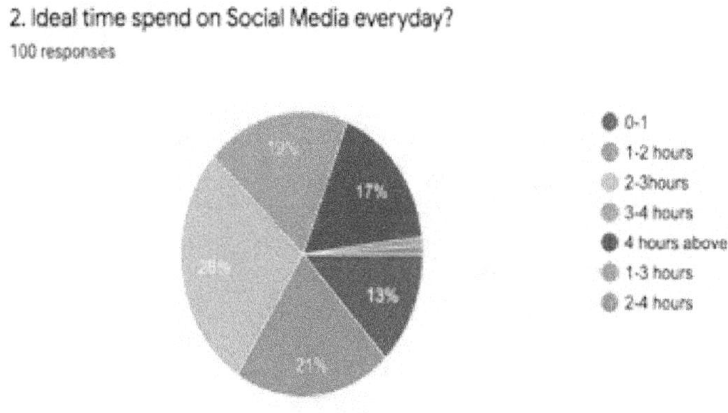

Fig 3

As shown in fig. 3 has been found that 28% of respondents spend 2-3 hours on social media, 21% 1-2 hours, 19% 3-4 hours,17% 4 hours or more, 13% 0–1-hour , rest 1% 2-4 hours,1-3 hours respectively.

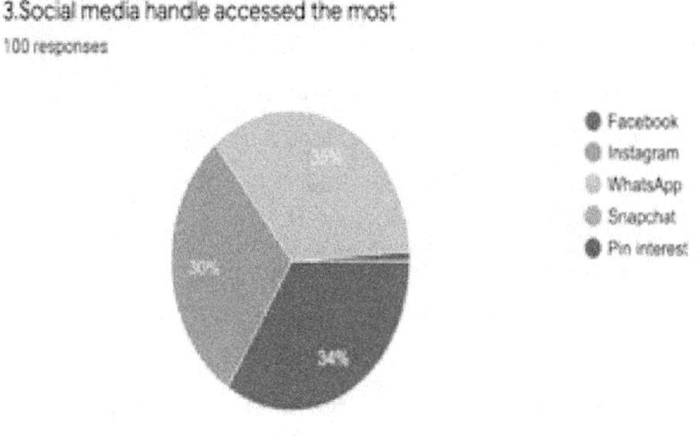

Fig 4

The study found that 34% of respondents are regular Facebook users, 35% use WhatsApp most often, 30% use Instagram, and the remaining 1% are pin interests. These are social media platforms that are very strongly recognized by the respondents showed in fig 4.

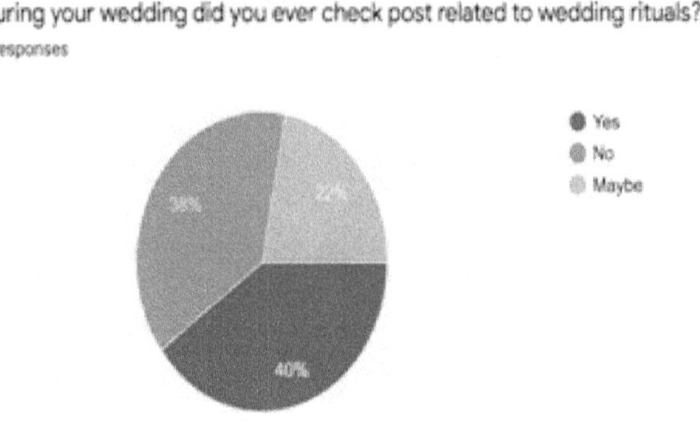

Fig 5

On being questioned about checking of posts related to wedding rituals 40% of respondents agreed that they used to see some posts directly or indirectly related to ideas that could be incorporated into a marriage or wedding. However, 38% did not mention any of the social media platforms, and the remaining 22% don't know if they've come across images, articles, ideas, videos, connected to weddings and marriages (Fig 5)

As represented in fig.6 below, the study found 62% of respondents sent their wedding invitations virtual while the remaining 38% did not use media as the invitation sending platform. The reason people use the virtual method to send wedding invitations is convenience and security. Needless to say, it is much more convenient to order invitations online from the comfort of your home instead of going to a store. Cost, personalization, RSVP tracking and eco-friendly. It was found that majority (82%) of the respondents did hire professional videographer and photographer rest 18% did not have hire any. Reason why people videographers and With a responsible and sincere photographer/ Videographer documenting your event, you can save energy, stress, and time. One can complete the work faster. The snapshots would be better. Having snapshots that tell the tale one can make more money in the long run than having them taken costs.

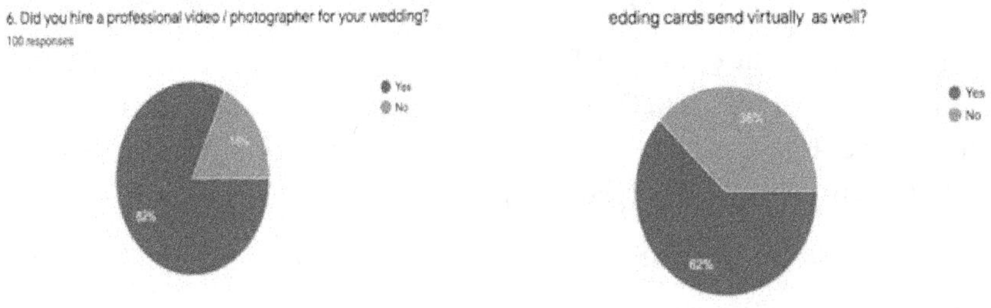

Fig 6 and Fig 7

As showed in the diagram below (Fig. 8), it was found that 78% of photos and videos were shared on various digital media platforms, while 22% did not share on any social platforms. Instagram, Snapchat, and Facebook are among the most popular platforms for sharing photos and videos. Couples share videos and photos for three main reasons: to provide others with valuable and exciting content, to show others a sense of who they are, and to strengthen and nourish their relationships because it makes them feel more connected to their partners. Internet users appreciate exchanging information if it helps them maintain existing relationships. Sharing information online can help people stay connected and establish connections. Since there is so much content in our lives and so many people to share it with, sharing is a beneficial way for users to manage their information.

The study found that on being asked which platform they prefer for sharing their posts

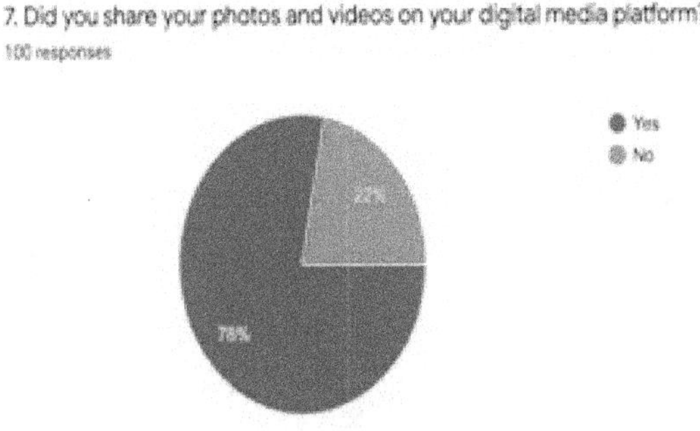

Enter Caption

be it pictures or videos, 69 percent out of 100% said they would share on Facebook, 51 percent out of 100% said they would share on Instagram, and 69 percent out of 100% said they would share on WhatsApp. The remaining 7 percent and 4 percent out of 100 said they would share on Snapchat and Pinterest, respectively is represented in the graph below (graph 1).

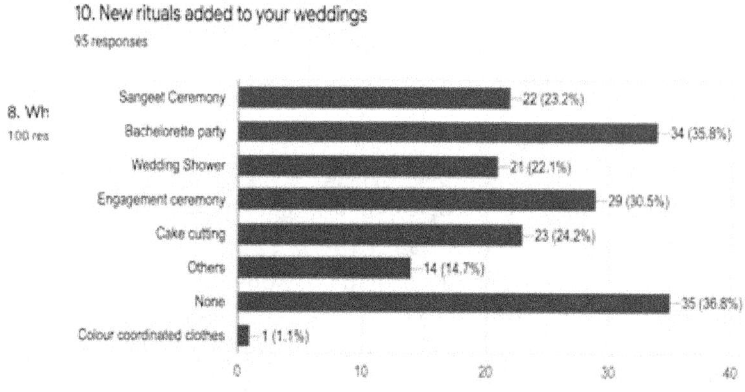

Graph 1

Through the data interpretations the diagram below (Fig. 9) represents that maximum (58%) respondents agreed that they did not add additional ceremonies to the wedding rites, while 29 percent agreed, and the remaining 13 percent were unsure.

From the data interpreted and represented in the below) it was found that 23.2 percent included a sangeet ceremony, 35.8% included a bachelorette party, 22.1 percent included a bridal shower, 30.5 percent included an engagement ceremony, and 24.2 percent included cake cutting. Other traditions were added by 14.7 percent and 36.8 percent of couples, respectively, while 1% added colour coordinated clothing, in which partners wore similar tones throughout their wedding ceremony.

It was found that majority(65%) of the respondents did not use hashtags as a countdown till date. Around 26% did use hashtags (#) rest 9% were not sure whether they have used it ahead of their wedding or D Day. Using a hashtag, on the other hand, makes it simpler to find them on numerous social media sites. Furthermore, your hashtag allows you to view photos as soon as they are posted by visitors, rather than having to wait 6-8 weeks for your photographer to return the photos or hunting down guests to see if there are any extra photos you want and then waiting for them to email them to you. The diagram given represents the data interpreted about using of hashtags in weddings.

The diagram below represents that majority of respondents (42%) used the trend of the countdown, 38% didn't use the trend, and 20% aren't sure or cannot remember whether they had the counting of days or not. Counting the remaining time for an anticipated event is something people do very often. Somehow, seeing the remaining time decreasing and seeing that it is decreasing gives us a positive feeling. It makes us feel as if we're getting close to what we're hoping for.

From the data interpreted and the diagram ,it was found that majority (76%) of the respondents did not add rituals because it was mentioned on Facebook, by their family and friends, 17% agree rest of 7% are unsure. It is seen that Couples, and brides, in particular, start using Facebook, Pinterest earlier than any other wedding site when they're in the planning mode. Over time, they move into decision-making mode and start to build a collection of images on Pinterest that will define their wedding.

According to some respondents, social media does have a huge impact on our decision-making. A large part of it comes from the peer pressure of making one's presence felt on social media, or else one risks becoming irrelevant. To keep up with "trends", we end up spending money on things that aren't so important. According to another, exposure to trends on social media leads to new wedding rituals that may serve as a catalyst, but are not entirely responsible. For example, some couples have given away plants as return gifts, but it hasn't caught on much. The new media has become a platform where we can see and adopt new cultures and ceremonies, according to some sections. Also, making your special day more special by including rituals is no harm, and it does not harm to have a positive outlook on social media. People tend to mimic what they see on social media platforms at a certain level. However, for some people it may not be the same for them, it also depends on their personality. A lot of recent weddings are affected by social media, causing financial and mental hardship to the couple and their family. Lastly, maybe it is due to peer pressure, we can blame digitization at times, but when it comes to wedding costs, it should not be based on such things, it cannot be justified at all, and couples can adjust their wedding costs accordingly.

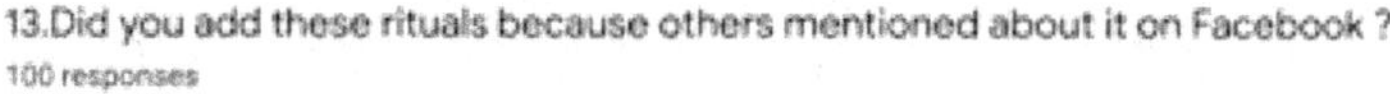

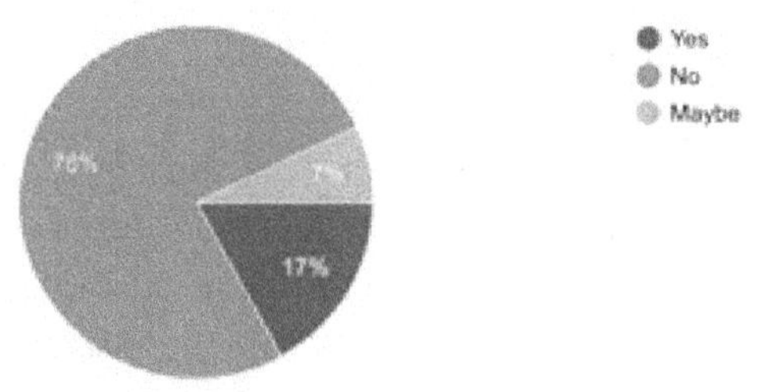

Majority of the respondents felt that It is up to us whether to include or not include the rituals. Again, if including them makes you feel happy and special, then everyone should choose their happiness. The pressure is only felt by those who put more emphasis on showing off than their happiness. In spite of this, some believe some might and some might not be based on how they react to the queries of including the new rituals in the event, as these are trending rituals which is why in one way or other things will be brought forward to the individual. Some stated that they had seen these posts on Facebook, so they wanted them in their wedding, too. However, when you look back on it, these new rituals do not seem to make much difference when you look back at how things were.

Conclusion

To summarise, the majority of respondents believe that while contemporary technology, particularly new media, has had a substantial influence on our lives, there has been little impact of new media on Changing Rituals and Impact Married Couples with special reference to Assamese weddings. Although some rituals were always part of the wedding, they were presented or done with a traditional touch. Some Rituals like Bachelorette party, bridal shower, sangeet ceremony, engagement ceremony, cake cutting, and so on. were seen now being included both traditional and modern touch. Social media has a significant influence on our decision-making. A major part of it stems from the peer pressure to have a social media presence or risk becoming irrelevant. We spend money on things that aren't as vital in order to stay up with "trends." According to another, exposure to social media trends leads to new wedding traditions, which may or may not be totally responsible. Making your big day even more unique by integrating traditions is also a good idea, as is maintaining a positive attitude on social media. At some level, people prefer to imitate what they see on social networking networks. For other people, though, it may not be the same; it also relies on their personality. Social media has impacted many recent weddings, creating financial and mental strain for the couple and their families. Finally, sometimes it is due to peer pressure, and we can sometimes blame digitalization, but wedding expenses should not be dependent on such factors; they cannot be justified, and couples should alter their wedding expenditures appropriately.The majority of those polled said that whether or not to incorporate rituals is up to us. Again, everyone should pick their happiness if involving them makes them happy and special. The pressure is only felt by individuals who value their appearance over their pleasure. Some said they saw similar posts on Facebook and wanted them in their wedding as well. Regardless, others feel that some might, and some might not be dependent on how they react to questions about integrating new rituals in the event, since they are trendy rituals, and so things will be pushed forward to the individual in some way.

Bibliography

Arnold, A. (2018, July 31). How Social Media Has Transformed The Idea And Costs Of The Ideal Wedding. Forbes.

Assam Wedding: Rituals, Traditions & Customs You Need To Know. (2020, October 20). Retrieved from Happy Weddings Blog: https://happyweddings.com/matrimony/blogs/assam-wedding-rituals-traditions-customs/

Barnes, M. W. (2014). Our Family Functions: Functions of Traditional Weddings for Modern Brides and Postmodern Families. 60-63.

Buckley, E. (2006). A Cross-Cultural Study of Weddings through Media and Ritual: Analyzing Indian and North American Weddings. McNair Scholars Journal, 10(1), 13-20.

Community, S. (2018, January 18). Wedding Hashtag Generator. Retrieved from https://www.shutterfly.com/ideas/author/shutterfly/

Dawn O. Braithwaite, Diana Breshears, Colleen Warner . (2009, January). Weddings. Encyclopedia of Human Relationships., 1-5.

Duttagupta, I. (2022, March 24). It's the social media era! This wedding season, luxe segments look up to Instagram for inspiration.

Irfan, A. (2021, July 31). #IDo: Does social media pressure ruin the joy of weddings? New Lifestyle.

Maheshwari, R. (n.d.). The Indian Wedding Industry and Use of Social Media. Dublin Business School, pp. 8-14.

Outlook. (2022, JAN 24). The Emerging Trend Of Planning Weddings Digitally With ShaadiWish.

SARVAIYA, N. (January 2020, January 22). How Indian weddings have evolved in the last decade. Vogue .

SUNADH, L. (Nov 2019, November 04). Shaadi Squad tells us why social media is important for wedding planning in 2019. Lifestyle Asia.

CHAPTER EIGHT

News Consumption Habits of Gen Z in India

Abhishek Roy[1], Academic Associate, IIMC Dhenkanal
Sanchar Marg, District: Dhenkanal, Odisha
Email: abhishek.roy.iimc@gmail.com
Pompy Paul[2], PhD Scholar, Assam University
Silchar, District: Cachar, Assam
Email: pompypaul1@gmail.com

Abstract

The Internet's potential as a catalyst in revolutionizing journalism as a discipline and practice has long been examined and contested. The development of digital media has recently generated concerns about the future of traditional media. The COVID-19 epidemic aggravated the conundrum when established newspaper publishers experienced a steep reduction in readership while digital platforms gained more popularity and dominance over the Indian media landscape. Not only has the Internet transformed how news is gathered and produced, but it has also altered how we consume and share the news. Arguably, the more simplified yet ever-connected network architecture of the internet in general, and social media specifically, has given rise to a novel yet inexpensive distribution system that has essentially accelerated the process of production, circulation and consumption of information in a neoliberal capitalist society. In light of all this, the study is an attempt to investigate into the pattern of news consumption of Generation Z, their general perception, and preference toward different mediums to acquire news in both traditional and digital media formats. The study uses Exploratory Sequential Design, a QUAL->quan mixed methods research approach which involves focused group interviews with young participants (age 18 to 25) and an elaborate online survey targeted towards young voters to provide insights into decoding the news consumption pattern of the Indian Gen Z.

Keyword: News Consumption, Gen Z, Media, Medium

Introduction

Electronics and information technology are two of the Indian economy's fastest-growing sectors. India has the world's fastest-growing newspaper market. Over the next five years, India's newspaper industry is projected to expand at a CAGR of 7.5% while the global newspaper market will essentially stay flat. More people are accessing online news as a result of lower broadband rates, faster internet speeds, and more affordable smartphones being available in India. According to FICCI and EY's annual report on the M&E sector, there were about 450 million online news subscribers between December 2019 and December 2020, comprising users of news portals, aggregators, and mobile apps. However, the number of daily regular users was significantly lower. This category includes about 57 per cent of Internet users. Nine out of ten of the most popular online newspapers are written in regional languages. Additionally, online news and magazine app downloads increased by 12% in 2020. According to a Forbes article, social media has eclipsed traditional media as the main source of news online, with more than 2.4 billion people using the internet. Instead of turning to traditional media, about 64.5 per cent of people now get breaking news from Facebook, Twitter, YouTube, Snapchat, and Instagram.

The internet has grown in importance as a source of information and knowledge for people from all walks of life. All of India's leading newspapers have launched e-papers and news websites. Online news is now available 24 hours a day, seven days a week. In many places of the world, it has advanced to the point where print media is being replaced by it. Online newspapers are becoming more popular among Indian newspaper readers. The online communication system is rapidly evolving. Accessing information that is available online has become simpler. You have a great deal of control over how you consume information thanks to the hyperlinks on news websites. Experts in new communication technologies predict that new media will remove numerous obstacles between viewers and information. New technologies are changing the way people read the news. Because of the participatory nature of the internet, people may effectively choose the news that interests them. Nowadays, leading newspapers of the world are shutting their print version and shifting to 100% digital websites. The effect of the Internet on the news industry could be in this term that nowadays digital websites are getting their space in newsrooms. This technological progress has also altered how users read to learn about certain events that are considered newsworthy, how they collect background knowledge on a specific development, or obtain information and express their opinions on it. Not to mention the brand-new revenue and advertising models that have evolved to support this digital information architecture.

Gen Z is the first generation of youth that grew up with a high level of media consumption. These young people grew up in a time of constant change, fast-paced news, of constant streaming services. Gen Z spends more time than any other generation watching TV, streaming films, playing video games, using social media, and posting about their lives on the Internet. This study was done to look at how individuals (between the ages of 18 and 25) who read online, consume information in general. It will illustrate how Gen Z respond to online news content and delivery and provide a better knowledge of the nature of Indian readers. Finally, this study will assist publishers of online material in tailoring their information to the needs of the intended audience and reader preferences.

Online News in India

The transformation of Indian media from print to broadcast to digital occurred later and at a slower pace than in the West. While India has seen a considerable increase in the number of online news outlets in recent years, this has been mostly due to traditional media outlets (newspapers and television networks) adopting digital platforms. In 1995, the prestigious newspaper "The Hindu" launched the country's first news website. In 1999, the Times of India Group, the country's largest media conglomerate, established IndiaTimes, its flagship internet webpage. Legacy media companies were not the only ones looking to cash in on the emerging internet; a number of technological companies saw the opportunity to commercialize media content online as well. For example, Rediff, an early Indian technology business started in 1996 that began by selling e-mail and e-commerce services, later evolved into a news portal and is still one of the country's most popular news websites today. India's media industry is at an interesting crossroads right now, as it has continued to thrive in the print and TV space while internet news has progressively gained traction. According to the Reuters Digital News Report 2019, the youth (under 35) population is driving this trend of online news consumption, reporting that they consume news online (56 per cent) much more than they do offline (print 16 per cent, television, 24 per cent). Television (38%) and the internet (34%) are almost equally essential news sources for older respondents. While internet news has grown in popularity in India, individuals appear to favour the online offerings of legacy brands. Even though a few digital-born sites appear as potential alternative news sources, legacy outlets such as NDTV, The Times of India, and even international channels such as the BBC outweigh them, according to the Reuters study.

The Commodification of 'News'

News has become a commodity, and it's a commodity that's not as easily understood by the public. But, like so many of the things we value, the news is more than just a way to deliver information – it's a complex human endeavour, and one that requires us to see the world from our own perspective. However, nowadays, the news is sold to consumers as a package, not unlike a box of cereal. The news, by definition, is essentially objective; it is only the observer who is subjective. But the media are a social construction, a set of institutions that are defined by the values of the people who run them. Hence, at times, objectivity itself becomes the tool of the status quo. We don't think about that fact, and that's one of the problems with the new media. We just want the news to tell us what we think we already know, thereby appealing to our confirmation bias. The reason the news media are considered to be "the fourth estate" is because of the power they hold in society. They represent the voice of the people – and the people they represent are powerful in a thriving democracy. However, the voice of the media is not as powerful as they think it is. The news media are simply not considered to be "the media" anymore. We are inundated with news every single day from both mainstream and alternative sources. We are constantly being fed "facts", but with the ever-changing and conflicting news that we are getting, it can be difficult to even have a semblance of integrity. The average reader will be shocked to discover that there is little difference between mainstream media and alternative media. They are one and the same. The mainstream media, for the most part, is funded by the corporations and government. They are only too happy to print whatever the government or corporation is saying, and it does not matter if they are in the public or private sector. So we see both sides of the media saying exactly the same things, and then we also get the fact that they all want to keep you distracted from the real news.

People do a lot of things with the help of the Internet these days. From ordering food to shopping, entertainment, education, gaming, and meeting for work. Our world now continues to revolve around the internet. Ever since the pandemic came, the Internet has become an inseparable part of our life. Just like food and water, communication is also a basic need of a human. The curiosity and need to know information, to be prepared for upcoming situations. A few decades back, newspapers and radio were the only mediums for mass communication, Television came much later. With the Internet, information began to spread with the speed of light, one piece of information reaches another part of the world in just one click. This has been an ongoing debate about whether 'news' is a commodity or a public good. If the news is a commodity then it will be served in such a way that users want to read, in a capitalist world, the consumer is the God. If the news is public good then those involved in bringing news to your newspaper will survive in an ever-competitive world. In 'news' as commodity side, Nick Tjaardstra, Director, Global Advisory at WAN-IFRA, says, "People are used to paying for newspapers. So in principle, paying for digital is nothing different." In Egypt where news is free until now but Tarek Atia, the founder of the Egypt Media Development Program, says "Publishers are struggling, revenue from online is going down and the value of banner ads is going down as well.

How has the Internet affected news consumption?

A report by Pew Research Center says, "People go to the Internet increasingly as a source ofinformation. Nearly half of all Internet users go to the Internet at least once every week to getinformation and use websites of television networks, national newspapers, cable news networks,and magazines."A study of print and web-based readers of The New York Times by Tewksbury and Althausfound that online readers were less keen to read international, national, and political stories thantheir print counterparts. Online readers are more focused on topics of personal interest.An article published by Forbes on changing habits of how we consume news and how socialmedia has changed talks about how Social media has become the main source of news onlinewith more than 2.4 billion internet users, nearly 64.5 per cent receive breaking news fromFacebook, Twitter, YouTube, Snapchat and Instagram instead of traditional media.

In a recent pollby Mint, over 50 per cent of Internet users indicated they first learn about breaking news on social media before hearing about it on the news, and 60% of the consumers share news via social media, messaging or email. Many internet users may spot breaking news on their feeds and visit news websites to learn more. According to the survey, traffic to news sites referred from social media increased by 57%. However, the amount of time people spend reading an article has decreased. The majority of individuals will just navigate through their newsfeed and come across relevant news items, but will only read the headlines or watch a little video clip of the piece. The average visitor will read an article for 15 seconds or less and will watch a video for 10 seconds on the internet. According to past studies, the informational needs of the digital end-user are extremely specialized, which seemed to be the industry's opinion at the time. Another study found that because there are so many free sites available these days, about 71% of website users would go somewhere else if they do not find what they are looking for on a given site.

The online newspaper paid subscriptions ranged from 0.2 per cent to 2.6 per cent of print circulation. According to the survey, just 2.5 per cent of users responded to premium material, and the majority had no intention of paying in the future at the time of the study due to the availability of free alternative news sources. The prominence of each social media site in the news ecosystem depends on two factors: its overall popularity and the extent to which people see news on the site. Reddit, Twitter and Facebook stand out as the sites where the highest portion of users are exposed to news – 67% of Facebook's users get news there, as do 71% of Twitter's users and 73% of Reddit users. However, because Facebook's overall user base is much larger than those of Twitter or Reddit, far more Americans overall get news on Facebook than on the other two sites. The future of journalism is being made on the Internet and online news will one day become mainstream journalism, according to Katz. Online news is dynamic and interactive because of technologies such as hypertext, and attractive because of ample use of multimedia. It provides 24×7 up-to-date information about local and international events to online users.

Generation Z and patterns of news consumption

Gen Z consumers may be pioneering a long-lasting change in news consumption. Young people can stay informed about social concerns and current events by using mobile devices, news alerts and notifications, and social media feeds. They are also becoming better consumers than their parents who were more likely to read newspapers and magazines in print. Gen Z is often a first-time internet user with an interest in a mobile lifestyle. With their interest in personalization, Generation Z is more willing to share data than previous generations, and they are interested in more than one kind of media. However, the trend is beginning to change. As a society, we are becoming increasingly aware of privacy and data breaches, which can limit personalized news feeds.

Young people are also making use of user-generated content formats and social media sites that emphasize images and videos to follow and engage with content producers who share their interests and frequently provide news and information. Some teenagers may live at home with Millennial or Gen X parents, who are more likely to have a pay TV subscription and whose news habits impact them, even though Gen Z consumers as a whole are less likely to favour watching TV in general. On the other hand, Gen Z adults, who are more likely to be in college, employed, and living alone and who are also less likely to subscribe to pay TV, only read one news source on average per day.Despite these differences, Generation Z is very connected and tech-savvy. The ways in which this young demographic consumes news present both opportunities and difficulties for news outlets and digital platforms.

Qualitative Approach:

According to the intended study, the key driver for Gen Z is a desire to receive personalized news based on their individual preferences. The intended study has traced the top 5 Gen Z news consumption behaviours by conducting onlinefocused-group interviews with 19 participants who fit the demography. Seven out of twelve participants are students while the other seven are individuals with jobs. Students from IIMC and JamiaMilliaIslamia studying media make up five of the twelve students that took part in the focused group interviews.Focused group interviews allowed the study to trace the varied patterns of consumption in an ever-expanding digital ecosystem and learn more about the choices and preferences of the younger generation of new media consumers.The following parallels in preferences were discovered after the qualitative assessment of the interview:

1. **Use mobile devices for news:**Gen Z is the first generation to grow up using mobile devices, which often come with built-in Internet access. For these young users, mobile devices are the centre of their daily lives. As per the results of the interview, 12 out of 19 Gen Z participants use mobile devices to access the internet, and they use them for an average of 8 hours per day. Many members of Gen Z favour smartphones over laptops and desktop PCs. The study found that younger persons were significantly more inclined to prefer mobile devices to desktops and laptops when it came to reading news. Tablet use is limited to only 3 Gen Z users that participated in the interview. Compared to their elder

counterparts, the younger members of Gen Z tend to utilise their mobile phones as their primary screen for searching news articles. "Mobility and interactivity have become the key features why our generation is more inclined towards digital devices. I mostly consume my news while commuting to work, or when I am taking my break. I do not have time to sit in front of the television, However, I do have this app, 'Public App' which helps me watch TV news on the go, and I have my sources sorted inside the app. So, I cut the clutter of traditional TV news and just consume whatever I want," said Bibhu, a PR practitioner in Bhubaneshwar.

2. **Subscribe to social media news feeds:** When it comes to social media news feeds, Gen Z is the first generation to grow up using them and continue to share content from the feeds on their social media accounts. According to the study, most Gen Z users (13 out of 19) have accounts on a social media network or use one regularly to view content and access social news feeds, but only 6 of them have a Facebook profile. Although it is not popular among Gen Z, a minority (3 out of 19) of them share content from the feeds on other social media networks. Gen Z consumers are also more likely to use their networks to share content than previous generations, which is a key driver for social media news feeds. Gen Z is also the first generation to have an interest in seeing the content from social networks and news feeds displayed on their social media news feed. The vast majority (13 out of 19) of Gen Z share content from their social media news feeds, with only (6 out of 19) of Gen Z saying they do not share content on their social media feeds. "Most of the time, we encounter news incidentally on social media, and we participate in whatever interests us and addresses our concerns. However, the internet does bring everything from everywhere and all at once, so it kind of drowns us in a vast ocean of information, most of which seems irrelevant to us and our informational needs, and hence, we tend to navigate through this huge pile of information by prioritising our preferences over other topics. Subscribing to certain sources that cater to our informational needs is one way to tackle that problem," said Prashant, who runs his own Digital Marketing firm in Delh.

3. **Get news and content through notification alerts:** Another popular Gen Z feature is using their smartphones and tablets to receive push notifications from social media networks and news feeds. According to the study, more than half (10 out of 19) of Gen Z consumers say they

check for notifications on their social media news feeds and receive content from sources they interact with daily. However, not all Gen Z users are getting notifications on their mobile devices. "Notification alerts are one of the most important changes to traditional newspaper business models over the last few decades," said Nikhil, anIIMC student, in a statement. "In today's news environment, it is not enough to simply publish news in a single form and wait for consumers to pick it up. News is now much more about interacting with consumers and giving them the information and news they want at the right time in order to create meaningful interaction,"Nikhil concluded.

4. **Participate in social media conversations:** Gen Z is more likely than previous generations to participate in social media conversations on social media networks, email, or online blogs and forums. Most Gen Z users (17 out of 19) participated in at least one social conversation in the last week. The study found that Gen Z also has a high interest in social media conversations. "It's not just participation. We also look at engagement and the different types of social media conversations happening online. Social media conversations are much more than just a conversation or even a chat. They give us insights on what are the concerns of the people, what interests them and how they indulge in public discourse on any given topic," said Nishat, a Journalism student atJamiaMilliaIslamia.

5. **Receive personalized news:** A key driver for Gen Z is a desire to receive personalized news based on their individual preferences. When considering news websites, social networks, news apps, newspapers, and other forms of digital news, Gen Z uses personalized, contextualized, and social features. Some news outlets are already catering to Gen Z. For instance, The Times launched an Instagram-driven augmented reality programme as part of a recently announced partnership with Facebook, which owns Instagram, in order to give consumers more customised and interactive experiences. The project will make use of Facebook's developer platform Spark AR, which provides access to a variety of tools and software required to build augmented reality filters and camera effects and then share them on Facebook and Instagram. The social media juggernaut is not involved in any editorial or storytelling choices but acts merely as a facilitator in interactive storytelling."The internet has transformed into an array of platforms and ways to communicate, with people communicating on one platform and sharing on another,"

said Ashish, who works in Newzera. "In today's digital news environment, companies that connect with consumers through different platforms are thriving and new and more innovative businesses are beginning to grow by finding unique ways to reach consumers using different forms of media," he added. "Consumers are demanding a consistent stream of news that reflects their interests, which is why we focus so heavily on social media and mobile," saidPritinanda, an intern in The Informist in Mumbai. "We are always learning how to reach our audience with a consistent level of quality, and provide the most personal and interactive experience possible for our readers. We all agree: We've hit the nail on the head this time, finding the secret to how young adults are receiving their news,"said Ashish. "We found that the most successful publishers were delivering what people want, which means providing personalized news that is relevant, timely, and accessible. But we also found that publishers are doing that at a large scale and this is something that needs to be embraced to help provide better services to society," he concluded.

Quantitative Approach

The 'quant' side of the study aims to investigate and quantify the subjective experiences of the participants in addition to the above qualitative insights that the 'QUAL' half of the study provided, and intends to draw conclusions by contrasting the results of both sides.The online survey approach was then used to determine how Indian Generation Z consumes news. It is a very common technique for researching Internet users. It is the systematic collection of audience data through emailing or posting questionnaires on messaging apps and social media. For this study, an online questionnaire was prepared with the help of Google Forms, and the online form link was sent via email and was also shared on social networking sites and instant messaging apps. For the purpose of the study,272 replies from respondents between the ages of 18 and 25 were collected and examined, and conclusions were made in light of the findings that the paper proceeds to discuss henceforth.

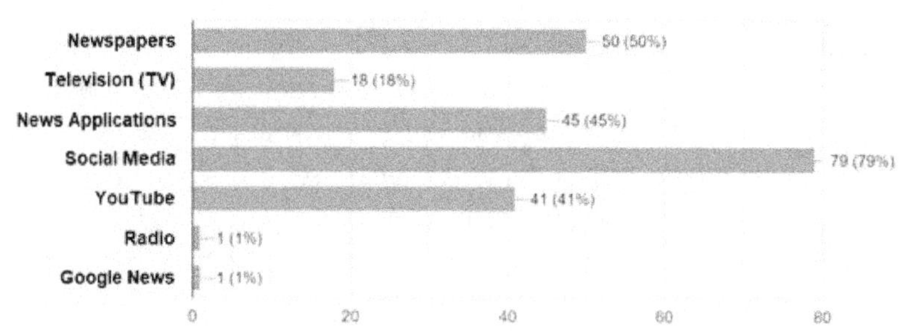

Fig 1

The above figure makes it apparent that social media (79%) and newspapers (50%) are the most popular news sources, followed by digital news apps (45%) and YouTube (41%).This demonstrates how social media is extensively used by around 80% of these young individuals. Interestingly, only 18% of respondents acquire their news via television.With over 476 million active social media users in India, traditional media sometimes lags behind when it comes to breaking news. People in today's fast-paced society cannot wait until the next day or turn on the television to learn about specific news. Smartphones with strong internet connections are useful in this situation.

Figure 2

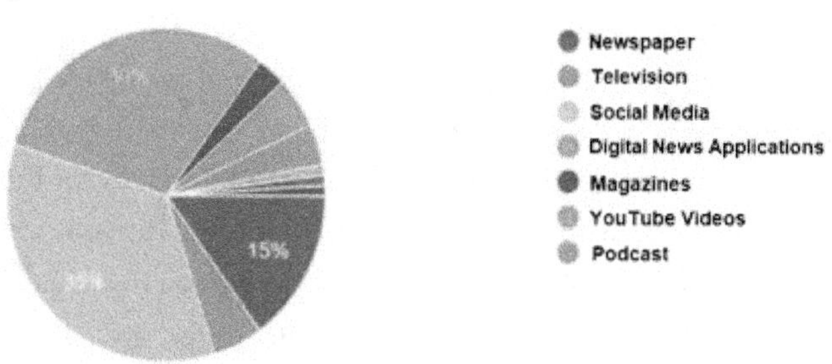

When it comes to reading about the "news in detail," around 40% of respondents choose socialmedia, followed by digital news applications which is 30%. Hence, it's obvious that youngsters don't waitfor the newspaper to come the next day and then read about the news. The fact that Social media incidentally, or algorithmically, delivers news content and allows public discussion around the news item at the same time, makes it more resourceful for the Gen Z to have a detailed understanding of a given event or development.

Figure 3

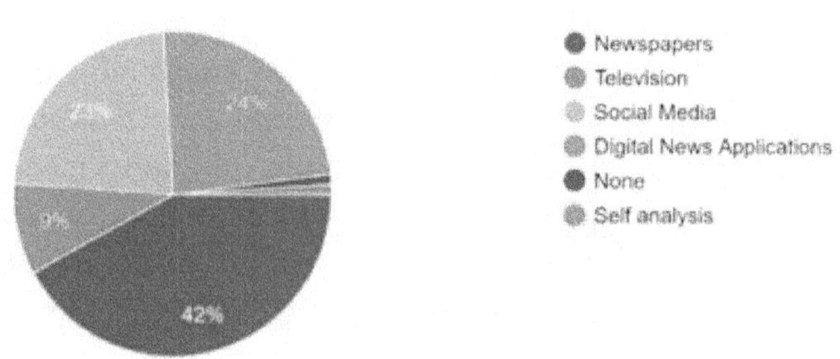

Reliability and authenticity of the information in the media business are critical to consumers.As more media outlets report on the information transmitted through social networks, people seek to learn about the sources of that information. They may take that knowledge as guidance for their own decisions. They may even try to control the information that appears on their own social media networks, using a variety of means. As per the above diagram, 42% of individuals think newspapers are the most reliable source of information when it comes to trustworthiness. Even though younger generations are embracing many new information-gathering methods and platforms like social media and YouTube, most people still trust the print media compared to any other media. Print media are followed by Digital news apps, which account for 24% of the market. Social media is also somewhere nearer to digital news apps, which amounts to 23% of the total responses gathered.In light of this, it can be said that social media sites like Facebook and Twitter are best suited for spreading news, while digital media continue to gain ground on print media in terms of market share. However, when it comes to trustworthiness, print media still has a significant advantage.

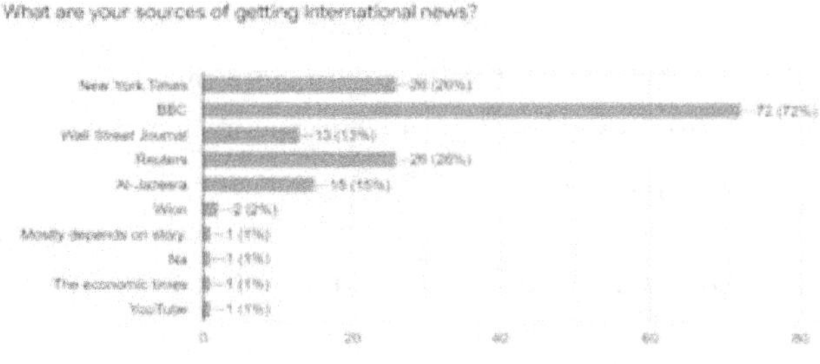

Figure 4

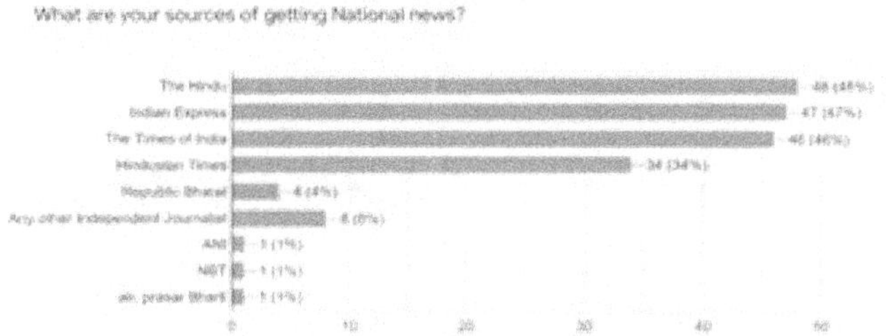

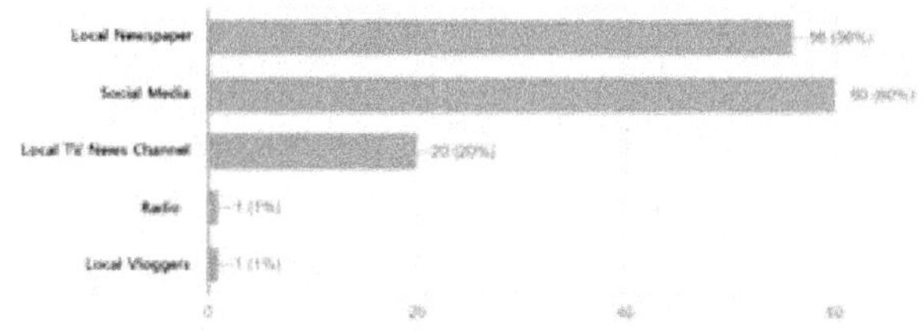

Figure 5

What are your sources of getting Local news?

Figure 6

It is clear in the above three charts that Indian news websites retain a separate section for global orInternational news, and people do follow international news websites to meet their informational demands. A total of 72% of survey respondents said they follow BBC news for world updates, with The New York Times and Reuters coming in second and third place, respectively, among Gen Z readers who follow global news.

The chart further demonstrates how traditional news outlets predominate online when it comes to national news. The Hindu (48%) was favored by the majority of respondents, followed by Indian Express (47%), The Times of India (46%), and Hindustan Times (34%). Only 8% of respondents said they follow independent journalists for news.When it comes to local news, 60% of those surveyed indicated they discovered local news on social media, while 56% of individuals obtain local news from local newspapers.

Figure 7

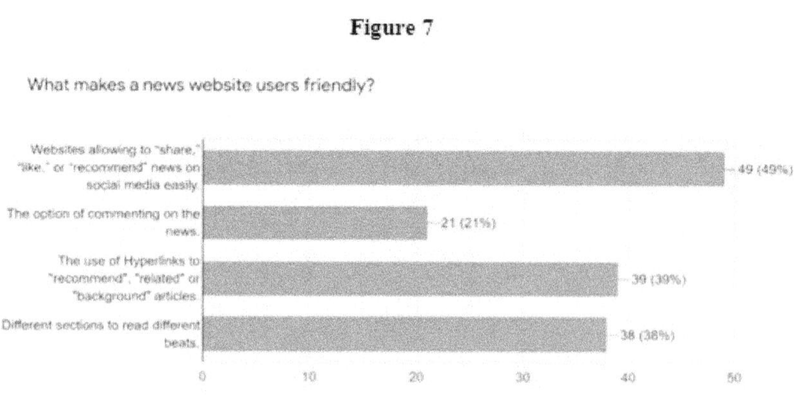

Out of total 272 respondents, 49% of them like the easy sharing option presented on an article while reading news on website or an app. Reading news on apps make it easy, otherwise it is quite difficult to share an article of newspaper to a long distance friend or on social network. People find reading online to be simpler, especially if the content is aptly categorized. It also helps the readers if they can read an item with just one click and obtain detailed coverage, background information, or any further information on the same page itself.

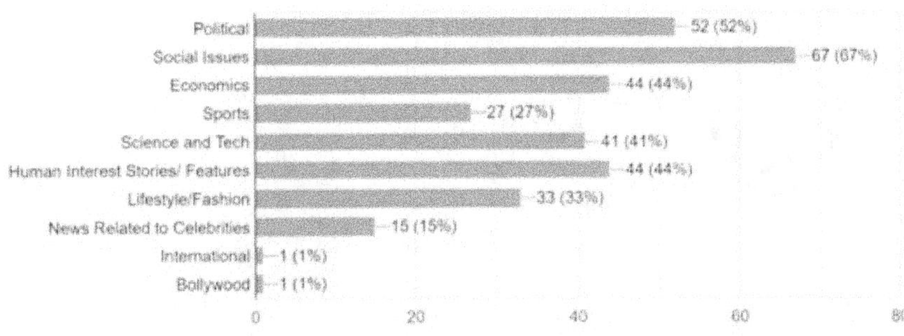

Figure 8

The reading preferences of new online readers in India are depicted in the above bar graph. The majority of respondents (67%) said they like to read about social issues, followed by politics (52%), economics and human interest stories (both 44%), science and technology (41%), and lifestyle and fashion (33%).

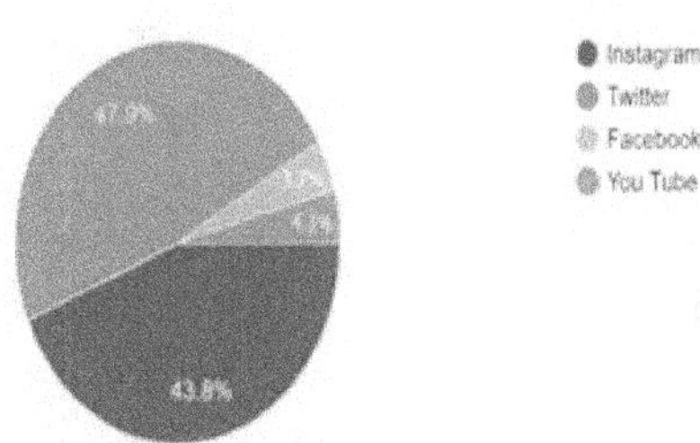

Figure 9

Nearly 90% of respondents name Twitter and Instagram as their preferred social media platform for consuming online news.To appeal and cater to this youthful demographic, news outlets (both mainstream and alternative) are increasingly extending their reach on Instagram.

Owning and operating a news website is competitive in today's climate. Therefore, the primary goal of a website is to attract users, whether they achieve this by creating an attention-grabbing title or by including an eye-catching image. Out of 272 respondents, 68% believe that creating a compelling headline will draw users to their website.

As can be seen from the pie chart above, 60% of respondents said they would prefer an ad-based model, in which they would not have to pay for the news but would instead see advertisements on the news organization's website, which would result in the news organization receiving money directly from advertisers. Only 34% of the 272 respondents who read the news online are willing to pay for it. Therefore, 60% of them will not pay for news.

Limitations of the study

The research figures are based on a survey of mostly English-speaking Indians who have access to digital devices; these users represent a small portion of a wider, more varied media market. In comparison to the larger Indian population, respondents are often wealthier, younger, and have a formal education. They are also more likely to live in cities.

Conclusion

Traditional media is facing a challenge as more and more people become connected to online outlets because of the real-time coverage.In addition, India is increasingly becoming a media market with a strong mobile focus, with a substantial portion of its population using smartphones and laptops to obtain news. As per the findings of this study, the majority of Indian readers prefer to read the most recent news, so currency is a deal-breaker. The majority of internet users have accounts on a variety of social media platforms. The notion that young people do not fully accept the news they read on social media, regardless of the fact that they consider it a significant source of information, is an intriguing aspect. Consumers in Generation Z are more concerned about cost and user experience. Focus group interviews assert that the majority of online readers demand constant updates and follow-ups. These days many readers acquire their news and information from social media, and hence, traditional media need to keep up to speed with online readership and not to be left behind.The study also highlighted that people on social media are very conversant with the way news is communicated online, both the format and presentation. Hence, journalists and news organisations need to have a social media presence in order to remain relevant, and they must always be aware of the latest communication technologies to stay on top. Hence, traditional news media outlets need to get their social media and digital marketing game up to reach a wider variety of audience hailing from different demographics. In addition, Individuals on Twitter prefer to get news and information from people on social media, and they are more likely to pay attention to a tweet or Facebook update that involves an organisation than a one from a random person. Another interesting and telling fact was that the majority of Twitter followers pay attention to tweets that are sent from a journalist, a business or a public figure on social media, while they pay little or no attention to content from unknown sources. Furthermore, readers were more likely to pay attention to a tweet or Facebook update sent from a known brand or personality than an account that they do not follow or which they had never heard about before.

Reference

Laghate, G. (2022, June 23). Indian M&E industry to grow at 8.8% CAGR to reach Rs 430,401 Cr by 2026: PwC. *The Economic Times.* https://economictimes.indiatimes.com/industry/media/entertainment/ media/indian-media-entertainment-industry-likely-to-touch-rs-4-30-lakh-cr-by-2026-pwc-report/articleshow/92410799.cms?from=mdr

Top 20 most popular newspapers in india by circulation. (n.d.). Retrieved September 3, 2022, from http://www.walkthroughindia.com/industry/ top-20-most-popular-newspapers-in-india-by-circulation/

Tewari P (2015) The Habits of Online Newspaper Readers in India. J Socialomics 4: 124.

doi:10.4172/2167-0358.1000124

Adgully Bureau. (2021, March 30). Online news audience grew to over 450 million in

2020: FICCI-EY report. *Adgully.Com.* https://www.adgully.com/online-news-audiencegrew-

to-over-450-million-in-2020-ficci-ey-report-102327.html

Martin, N. (2021, December 10). How Social Media Has Changed How We Consume

News. *Forbes.*

https://www.forbes.com/sites/nicolemartin1/2018/11/30/how-social-media-has-changedhow-

we-consume-news/?sh=9b0c4663c3ca

Shearer, E., &Matsa, K. E. (2020, August 27). News Use Across Social Media Platforms

2018. *Pew Research Center's Journalism Project.*

https://www.pewresearch.org/journalism/2018/09/10/news-use-across-social-mediaplatforms-

2018/

Madhukalya, A. (2020, April 21). India's internet consumption up during Covid-19

lockdown, shows data. *Hindustan Times.* https://www.hindustantimes.com/indianews/

india-s-internet-consumption-up-during-covid-19-lockdown-shows-data/story-

ALcov1bP8uWYO9N2TbpPlK.html

Contributor, W. E. (2020, July 28). News as a commodity – How newspapers can survive

the digital age. *WAN-IFRA.* https://wan-ifra.org/2018/03/news-as-a-commodity-hownewspapers-

can-survive-the-digital-age/

33

Ravindran, Raveena(2021). *News Consumption Pattern among the Youth during*

Lockdown. KristuJayanti Journal of Humanities and Social Sciences. Vol. 1, Issue 2

(2021).

Adgully Bureau. (2021, March 30). Online news audience grew to over 450 million in

2020: FICCI-EY report. *Adgully.Com.* https://www.adgully.com/online-news-audiencegrew-
to-over-450-million-in-2020-ficci-ey-report-102327.html

How Gen Z redefines media consumption habits—Think with Google APAC. (n.d.). Think with Google. Retrieved September 3, 2022, from https://www.thinkwithgoogle.com/intl/en-apac/consumer-insights/consumer-trends/stay-woke-how-gen-z-teaching-us-about-future-news-and-information/

News at their fingertips: Digital and social tech power Gen Z teens' news consumption. (n.d.). Deloitte Insights. Retrieved September 3, 2022, from https://www2.deloitte.com/xe/en/insights/industry/technology/gen-z-news-consumption.html

Selligent. (2022, May 12). *50% Gen Zers say they have control over their personal data.* GlobeNewswire News Room. https://www.globenewswire.com/news-release/2022/05/12/2441507/0/en/50-Gen-Zers-say-they-have-control-over-their-personal-data.html

Kurzer, R. (2018, September 11). *Report: Gen Z, Millennials more willing to give up personal data in exchange for personalized experiences.* MarTech. https://martech.org/report-gen-z-millennials-more-willing-to-give-up-personal-data-in-exchange-for-personalized-experiences/

LaRoses and Diddi, (2006, June). Getting Hooked on News: Uses and Gratifications and
the Formation of News Habits Among College Students in an Internet Environment.
Journal of Broadcasting & Electronic Media June 2006.

Issawi, D. (2020, October 31). As augmented reality evolves, the reporting is all around you. *The New York Times.* https://www.nytimes.com/2020/10/31/insider/times-augmented-reality-Instagram.html

Stroud, Natalie Jomini, Scacco, Joshua, and Curry, Alex. (2014, March). Analysis of News
Sites. *Center for Media Engagement.* https://mediaengagement.org/research/news-site-analysis/

Althaus, S. L., & Tewksbury, D. (2000). Patterns of Internet and traditional news media use in a networked community. *Political communication, 17*(1), 21-45.

Jha, L. (2022, June 15). *Over half of Indian users consume news on social media.* Mint. https://www.livemint.com/industry/media/over-half-of-indian-users-consume-news-on-social-media-11655305366849.html

CHAPTER NINE

Localizing the Global and Globalizing the Local in the context of the Northeast

Dr. Mohsina Rahman

Assistant Professor

Department of Mass Communication and Journalism

Assam Women's University

mohsina.rahman643@gmail.com

Abstract

Globalization has become a buzzword in the present context. It has reduced the barriers in the flow of information and provided greater exposure to the world and beyond. New markets, MNCs, media networks, the globalnetwork of NGOs,global trade agreements, and the export and import of goodsare all because of globalization. It has bought a homogenized culture within the local cultures which leads to convergence rather than divergence as the consequence of modernization,such as "McDonaldization" or"Coca Colonization". The Northeast region has access to foreign markets such as Bhutan, China, Bangladesh and Myanmar. The region is also rich in fertile soil and people's potential to work for the betterment. Despite this huge potential, the conventional market hinders poor infrastructure, unemployment, connectivity, insurgence problems, etc. The Northeast of India comprises eight states, and each state has a central university, with Assam having two central universities. Technology's growth has shifted from national and state education to global education, from teacher-centric to learner-centric education. E-learning is the fastest process of learning globally. Most of the central universities of India are entering into tie-ups with foreign universities for mutual exchange of programs, intending to increase the cooperation between Indian and foreign academic institutions, offer additional choices to students and; improve curriculum, knowledge and educational content.This paper exploresthe positive and negative consequencesof local cultures of the Northeastdue to globalization and the role ofcentral universities in promoting cultures of the Northeast globally through their websites.

Keywords: Northeast culture, Glocalization, websites of central universities promoting culturesof Northeast.

Aims

To study the consequences of local cultures of the Northeast due to globalization and the role of central universities in promoting cultures of the Northeast globally through their websites.

Objectives

1. To study the positive and negative consequences of globalization on local cultures of the Northeast.
2. To study whether the websites of the central universities of the Northeast promote the culture and language of their state through their websites.

Methodology

The study is based on secondary data collected from various journals, books, magazines, and relevant online sources related to the topic. It is also an analytical study as the analysis and evaluation of the websites werestudied for the purpose.The homepages of thewebsites of all the universities were studied. The study defined two parameters for the study of culture and tradition of the Northeast through the websites. The parameters used for the study were:

1. **Language:** Language is one of the important features of the website. Language expresses the ideas and customs within different cultures and societies. A website should be developed with a facility to change language according to the user's convenience. The websites nowadays are mostly bi-lingual or multi-lingual, where English is used as the parallel language. Here it is seen whether the central universities of the Northeast have the respective state language on their website for the globalization of the culture through the websites.

2. **Pictures:**University's website can offer a natural link between local culture and the world of ideas. One such link can be pictures and videos. Love for the state and local community through pictures can provide a space for contact with the globalization of the culture.

Globalization and Glocalization of cultures in Northeast India

Globalization refers to integrating different economic, political, and socio-cultural systems worldwide. Globalization can also be termed as a process of increasing global socio-economic interdependence through increased exchange of goods and services, capital and technology, as well as global interaction and interconnectedness of people and culture. Globalization, in otherwords, is the process through which the diverse world is unified into a singlesociety. (Kazi, 2022)

Globalization has positive and negative effects on a region's or a country's cultural diversity. In a globalized society, a specific group or region's culture is evolving due to increased interaction with other cultures—moreover, culture changes due to changing socio-economic and political situations. "People make culture, culture produces people," Tomlinson (1999) remarked.

Globalization has impacted the cultures of Northeast India. The culture of the Northeast is spread to a different parts of the world. Globalization has opened the door for the Northeast region to adapt to the western culture of highly developed nations from different parts of the world. Technology's growth has shifted from national and state education to global education, from teacher-centric to learner-centric education. E-learning is the fastest process of learning globally. Research has shown that Asian countries have a 46% increase in internet users than all other continents (Internet World Stats, 2019). Technology alone does not necessarily enhance education, yet a mix of teaching strategies and technological innovations can create unique and successful learning environments. Also, because of globalization, some superstitious beliefs are prevalent in the Northeast, especially in Assam, where most women and sometimes men are considered witches and killed, raped, beheaded, raped, and forced-fed excreta by raging mobsare minimized because of globalization. This type of practice was mostly among the low literacy rate in the region, high superstitious beliefs, lack of a proper health care system and also because of the outspoken nature of the women. Due to globalization, these issues were raised on global platforms where women can raise their voices against those atrocities. Traditional folk dances, music, art, literature and artefacts were showcased before the world about the richness of the Northeast in its culture and tradition. Heirloom Naga is a design firm from Nagaland. It has been instrumental in showcasing "MadeinNagaland" textiles to customers within the country and a very discerning clientele in several countries. Daniel Syiem is an ethnic fashion house inShillong. It is uplifting the traditional fabrics of the Northeast, mainly Meghalaya and promoting its use and innovating it in modern, contemporary and international fashion. Designer Sanjukta, known for designing beautiful Mekhela Chador and reviving the silk of Assam, showcased her new collection,"Alphool" at the New York Fashion Week, 2022, on Feb 12. At the same time, globalization is also localizing western culture in various ways, such as designing western outfits using the traditional silk of Assam.

Cinema in North East India works as a tool for bringing the 'seven sisters into the global platform.Northeast India is linguistically and culturally diverse; many such stories can be portrayed in such diversity. Again, some of the stories of the Northeast now travel to almost every film festival globally. Cinemas of these regions are seen showcasing the essence of originality and uniqueness.Again while talking about Glocalization, the "Hip Hop" culture has taken the world by storm, where local youths are seen altering the western culture to match their taste with their local culture.KFC, Starbucks, and Taco Bell rolled-out stores in the Indian market with the taste of the local requirements. Beers like the North-East IPA and the West Coast IPA are quintessentially American flavoursthat have been matched with the local taste. Netflix, a television and movie streaming service, operates in most countries worldwide but has localized its shows country-wise.

Many people worldwide know about the Bihu dance and Bihu songs of the Assamese, Bagrumba and Bordoisikhla of the Bodo, Laiharawa of the Manipuri and Gumrag dance of the Missing. Traditional foods and their medicinal value have attracted interest world-wise, which has resulted in the commercialization of those products with a good market value. Globalization also plays an important role in the traditional skill and knowledge of the tribal and ethnic groups. It has provided them a platform to show their talents at national and international levels. North-East is a beautiful place referred to as 'seven golden crystals' like any part of 'incredible India' (e.g. Kerala, Jaipur, etc.) and is a wonderful tourist attraction. Tourism and cultural heritage arealso other positive and profitable impacts of globalization. Nowadays, more and more tourists from distant places come to visit North East Indiaand enjoy the scenic beauty of this region. The region offers them various wildlife, mountaineering, trekking, culture and tradition and a host of other adventures.Northeast India is home to wildlife sanctuaries like Kaziranga National Park, famous for the one-horned rhinoceros, Manas National Park, Nameri, Orang, DibruSaikhowa in Assam, Namdhapha in Arunachal Pradesh, Balpakram in Meghalaya, KeibulNamjao in Manipur, Intanki in Nagaland, Khangchendzonga in Sikkim. Globalization gives ample employment opportunities and avenues in these sectors.

Globalization has its negative impacts too. Western cultures have diffused the tradition and habits of the people of the Northeast. Youngsters nowadays tend to have an attraction towards the foods of the west, such as KFC, McDonald's etc., and s a result, the traditional food habit is declining day by day. Globalization has also affected the languages of the North Eastern tribes. Various ethnic dialects of indigenous tribes are now endangered due to the mixture of foreign languages. Accumulating various foreign languages tends people to forget about their own indigenous culture.

Study of the websites of the central universities of the Northeast

The government of India has decided to establish as many as seven central universities under its direct funding to ensure that the region gets the best education, which might contribute further to enhanced employment opportunities in the region. The main aim of the university is not just to enable students to excel in the field of knowledge but also has its more significant role in national development, bringing social change to society at large, and developing a sense of morality in the community (Mittal, 2010, p. 266). North East India is one of the most culturally diverse areas of the world. The culture of the northeastern states is characterized by the diverse ethnic groups settled in the region. Each tribe has its distinct custom, tradition and beliefs.The Northeast of India comprises eight states, and each state has a central university, with Assam having two central universities.The website of an institution, generally speaking, is the representative or flagship of the institution that seeks to communicate the organization's mission, vision, values and cultures. It contains, in other words, the information which, in earlier times, a prospectus used to provide about the organization.Academic websites are a better medium to impart education worldwide.These universities can also be a better medium for globalizing the unique culture of the Northeast.

List of Central Universities of Northeast

1. Assam University
2. Tezpur University
3. NEHU
4. Nagaland University
5. Sikkim University
6. Mizoram University
7. Rajiv Gandhi University
8. Tripura University
9. Manipur University

Homepages of the websites of the central universities
1. Homepage of Assam University

The site offers information only in one language, i.e. English. Links for language Hindi, Assamese, and other multi-lingual languages are missing. No images or videos of the state's culture and heritage are seen.

2. Homepage of Tezpur University

The site offers information only in English and Hindi. Links for language Assamese and other multi-lingual languagesare missing.No images or videos of the state's culture and heritage are seen.

3. Homepage of NEHU

The site offers information only in English and Hindi. Links for language Khasi and other multi-lingual languagesare missing. No images or videos of the state's culture and heritage are seen.

4. Homepage of Nagaland University

The site offers information only in one language i.e. English. Links for various languages of the state and other multi-lingual languages are missing. On the top of the homepage, the symbol of arrows can be seen, which is a part of Naga culture.

5. Homepage of Sikkim University

The site offers information only in English and Hindi. Links for Multilingual language are missing. On the top of the homepage, images of the Himalayas can be seen, which can help promote tourism in the state.

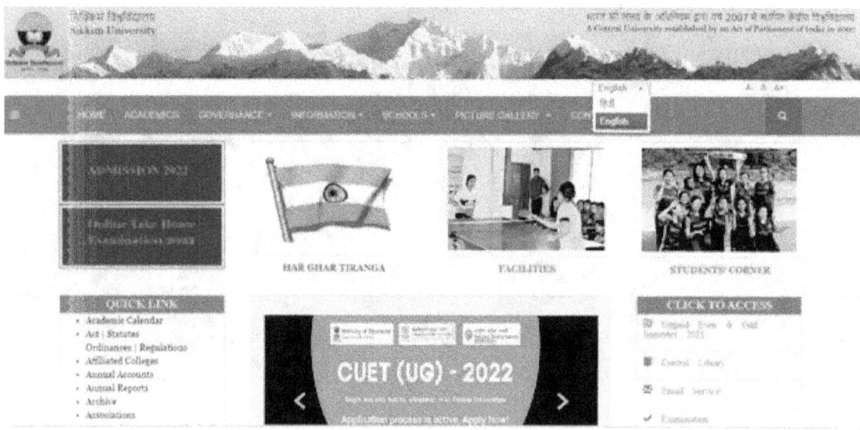

6. Homepage of Mizoram University

The site offers information only in English and Hindi. Links for language Mizo and other multi-lingual languagesare missing. No images or videos of the state's culture and heritage are seen.

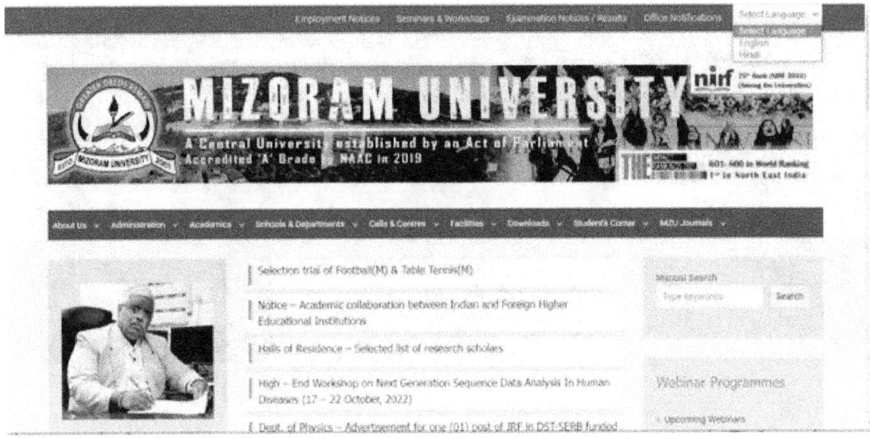

7. Homepage of Rajiv Gandhi University

The site offers information only in English and Hindi. Links for multi-lingual languagesare missing. No images or videos of the state's culture and heritage are seen.

8. Homepage of Tripura University

The site offers information only in English and Hindi. Links for language Bengali and other multi-lingual languagesare missing. No images or videos of the state's culture and heritage are seen.

Visit of His Excellency Mr. Kenji Hiramatsu, Ambassador of Japan to India in T.U.

9. Homepage of Manipur University

The site offers information only in English and Hindi. Links for language Manipuri and other multi-lingual languagesare missing. No images or videos of the state's culture and heritage are seen.

Findings and Conclusions

The universities are time to time, arrange talks and discussions on the culture and tradition of their states, and they are in tie-ups with foreign universities for mutual exchange of programmes, but negligence participation in promoting the cultures of the Northeast is seen from the websites of these universities. The website acts as a bridge between the users and the world of information available on the internet. In the age of ICT, the website is the primary source of information for an institution to disseminate and provide access to information to the clientele. However, in our study, most universities have failed to construct websites with regard to the culture and tradition of the region.

Only Nagaland University and Sikkim University have local or cultural identities regarding the university's symbols or settings on their websites. In most universities,the local or cultural identities are missing in virtual toursor symbols. For instance,Tezpur University is located in a beautiful natural environment from where great Himalayan ranges can be seen shining in a silver lining.

In a country like India, where people speak different languages, websites should be developed at least in three languages, the national language, i.e. Hindi; the official language, i.e. English and the local language of the state concerned. Indian culture has been the research topic for many western scholars because of its diversity in language and cultural ingredients. But most of the universities' websites allow access to websites in English and Hindi. Also, some of the websites of the central universities use English only and no other language.

Recommendations

1. Universities of the Northeast should focus on developing their website to globalize the region's culture.
2. The government should take several steps to safeguard the traditions and cultures of the people living in the area.
3. Traditional skills and knowledge of the indigenous tribe should be preserved in every possible way.

References

1. Baral, K. C. (2006).Globalization and Tribes of Northeast India.IndianFolklife, 22,3-5.
2. Roudometof, V. (2016). Glocalization: A critical introduction. London: Routledge.
3. McLuhan, M. 1964. Understanding Media. London: Routledge.

4. Das, N. (2015). A Study on Globalisation and Ethnic Women of North-East India. *International Journal of Humanities & Social Science*, IV(I), 76-79.

5. T. Jacob, Thomas. 1993. Indian Tribal Culture: A Rediscovery of Gospel Values.*Indian Journal of Theology*, 35(2), 64-76.

6. Grigorescu, A., &Zaif, A. (2017). The concept of Glocalization and its incorporation in global brands' marketing strategies. *International Journal of Business and Management Invention*, 6(1), 70-74.

7. Jena, P. K. (2010). Indian Handicrafts in Globalization Times: An Analysis ofGlobal-Local Dynamics. *Interdisciplinary Description of Complex Systems* 8 (2) ,119-137

8. Rajyalakshmi, P; (1999) "Tribal Food Habits", *Gian Publishing House*, New Delhi110002.

9. Tomlinson, J. (1999). Globalization and Culture. Chicago, IL: University ofChicago Press.

10. Gharphalia, M. (2018). Impact of globalization on the society and culture of NE India. *International Journal of Research and Analytical Reviews*, 5(1).

CHAPTER TEN

Exposure to Cartoon Programmes and its Impact on School Going Children

Maria Belsiya A[1], Dr. Arul Selvi G[2]

(1) Academician

(2)Assistant Professor, PG and Research Department of Visual Communication,

Holy Cross College, Tiruchirappalli

Abstract

In today's world Children without smart phone is not imaginable, it became an inherent part of their life. Children are trapped in the illusion of Cartoon Channel, the current generation have grown a lot smarter than the generation which existed a decade ago. Earlier, the content of cartoons programs and the visual effects did not involve the kids in day to day life but now it does. They start to watch cartoon at the age of 2 when their mind starts to grow, they have such a curiosity on what they see, so they observe and learn fast. Watching cartoon helps them to wide open their knowledge. In this context, a study is conducted by the researcher on school going students in district of Trichy based on a sample of 100 (3rd and 5th standard students). The survey method was used to select samples and questionnaire was used as a tool to collect data from the students. The main objective of this study that the visuals in the cartoon helps them to create fantasy and improve imagination and to find out the Cartoon character helps children to understand others in their facial expression.

Keywords: Cartoon, Iillusion, Visual, Effects, generation

Introduction

The child, who was born in the 90s in India, had limited options for entertainment. Subsequently television dominated with serialized cartoons on channels like cartoon network, Disney Junior, Discovery Kids, Pogo TV, Hungama TV, Chutti TV and so on. Even today in the OTT (Over- The-Top) platform like Netflix and Disney+. According to Internet and Mobile Association of India (IAMAI) Children between the age of 5 to 11 years are the 15% of India's active internet users which means 66 million. Watching cartoon means getting into a fictional world. The illustration of realistic and semi-realistic stuffed with full of fun and unimaginably vision.

What is Cartoon

It comes from Italian word Cartoon, which simply means a large sheet of paper or a card, the material on which drawing is made. It refers funny drawing or animation of Illustration in an unrealistic or semi realistic style. An image or series of images for satire, caricature, humor, motion picture that relies on a sequence of illustrations for its animation the first sense is called cartoonist and the second sense is called animator.

Positive Effects

They laugh when they laugh so gives good blood circulation. When they don't like to eat certain vegetables or fruit by seeing the cartoon character, they intake like sailor man the famous cartoon character gets power and energy by eating spinach. Audio- visual learning created great impact then traditional method of learning. At the age of 2-5 child can't read but allow to their mind on whatever they see and hear. So, the colorful visual of cartoon program and the funny voices of cartoon attracts them a lot. They remember the concept for long time when they learn with cartoonist Image. They learn to respect the elders as the cartoon character does. Many of the cartoon series are in different languages so it enhances the learning of new language. When their favorite cartoon character is loyal and share everything after school children apply into his day-to-day life.

Negative Effects

They learn abusing words, way to cheat, less physical activity, aggressive, fighting, very easily diverge from reality, more into illusion world, isolated from friends and neighbors, loss of vision, violent, screen addiction, health issues, eating and sleeping habit, anti-social behavior and so on.

Review of Literature

Rezan Karakas (2012) findings imply that if a picture save a thousand words then draw a picture and save a thousand words. The cartoon can be used to develop the skills and understand the explanation. Cartoon videos either long or short helps to increase the student's vocabulary skills also develops their critical thinking.

Maryam Khaleghipour, Ehsan Shahghasemi (2020) stated that, one of the most important behaviors of children is imitation which helps to improve their cognitive level and increase their understanding of emotions and challenges in various situations.

'The Effect of Cartoons on Children' (2016) since children are attracted by cartoons that directly or indirectly shape their Behavior. This study further revealed, by the age of 3, children become heavy-viewers. It also explained that there is some positive effect of the cartoon on children, such as they help in language, moral and mental development of children. This study further revealed that children become aggressive after watching the cartoon and they started behaving like their favorite cartoon characters in their real life too.

Dharmendra Kumar(2018) Says that different age group and gender get in different way by the content of cartoon. They reflect the influence of cartoon watching in day-to-day life. Watching cartoon has more positive impact on students like eating habits among students, social sensibility, learning, imitate their favorite cartoon character and also they learn how to solve their problem.

Research Method

The survey method method was used to select samples for the survey and questionnaire was used as a tool to collect data from the students. The data collected from aged from 7 to 11 years the questions were explained individually and collected the data. IPM SPSS 23 software was used to do the statistical test such as frequency tests and t-Test were done to analyze the data.

Objectives Of The Study

- To study what do the children learn by watching cartoon.
- To find out visuals in the cartoon helps them to create fantasy and improve imagination.
- To find out that the Cartoon character helps children to understand facial expression

Hypothesis

- Visuals in the cartoon helps them to create fantasy and improve imagination.
- Cartoon character allows the children to understand the feelings through facial expression.
- Watching cartoon helps children to develop their communication skills and influence them in education.

Analysis And Interpretation

Frequency test were conducted to know which medium is preferred by the school going children to watch cartoon and also to know for what purpose they watch cartoon, the results were tabulated.

Frequency Tests

Table -1 Watch Cartoon in Mobile

		Frequency	Percent	Valid Percent	Cumulative Percent
Valid	always	59	59.0	59.0	59.0
	often	41	41.0	41.4	100.0
	Total	100	100.0	100.0	
Total		100	100.0		

The above table shows that respondents who watches cartoon in mobile. Out of 100 cases 59% always watches cartoon in their mobile phone, 41% often watches cartoon in their mobile phone.

Table -2 Watch Cartoon for Education

		Frequency	Percent	Valid Percent	Cumulative Percent
Valid	always	63	63.0	63.0	63.0
	often	31	31.0	31.0	94.0
	sometimes	6	6.0	6.0	100.0
	Total	100	100.0	100.0	

Out of 100 cases 63% always watch cartoon for education purpose, 31% often watches cartoon for education purpose as well as 6% sometimes watch cartoon for education purpose.

Table -3 Watch Cartoon for Entertainment

		Frequency	Percent	Valid Percent	Cumulative Percent
Valid	always	63	63.0	63.0	63.0
	often	34	34.0	34.0	97.0
	sometimes	3	3.0	3.0	100.0
	Total	100	100.0	100.0	

In the total number of 100 cases 63% always watch cartoon for entertainment, 34% often watches cartoon for entertainment as well as 3% sometimes watch cartoon for entertainment.

Testing Hypothesis

One way ANOVA,post hoc test and t-Test were done for testing the hypothesis,

1. Cartoon character allows the children to understand the feelings through facial expression.
2. Cartoon visuals helps them to create fantasy and improve imagination.
3. Watching cartoon helps children to develop their communication skills and influence them in education and the result were tabulated.

1. Cartoon character allows the children to understand the feelings through facial expression.

Table -4 One way ANOVA

S.no	Dependent Variable	Always	Sometimes	Rarely
1	Cartoon allows you to understand the feelings through facial expression	2.43	1.20	1.00

Table -5 Post hoc test

S.no	Dependent Variable	F value	Sig.value	Degrees of freedom between groups (df)	Degrees of freedom within groups (df)
1	Cartoon allows you to understand the feelings through facial expression	10.369	.000	2	97

A one-way ANOVA was done with " Get inspired by Cartoon Character" as the independent variable and recoded as Cartoon Character with three groups namely Always,Sometimes and Rarely and dependent variable "Cartoon allows you to understand the feelings through facial expression" is significant.

Table -5 shows F(2,97)=10.369; p=.000.

A post hoc test was done where childrenalways allow Cartoon character (M=2.43) to understand the feelings through facial expression and those who allows sometimes(M=1.20) and Rarely(M=1.00). Table -4.

2. Cartoon visuals helps them to create fantasy and improve imagination.

Table -6 One way ANOVA

S.no	Dependent Variable	Always	Sometimes	Rarely
1	Cartoon helps to create fantasy	2.33	1.60	1.20
2	Cartoon helps to improve imagination level	2.11	1.20	1.11

Table -7 Post hoc test

S.no	Dependent Variable	F value	Sig.value	Degrees of freedom between groups (df)	Degrees of freedom within groups (df)
1	Cartoon helps to create fantasy	9.753	.000	3	96
2	Cartoon helps to improve imagination level	3.652	.012	3	96

A one-way ANOVA was done with " Get inspired by Graphic Elements" as the independent variable and recoded as Graphic Elements with three groups namely Always,Sometimes and Rarely and dependent variable "Cartoon helps to create fantasy" is significant.

Table -7 shows $F(3,96)=9.753$; $p=.000$.

A post hoc test was done where children always allow Cartoon character (M=2.33) to understand the feelings through facial expression and those who allows sometimes(M=1.60) and Rarely(M=1.20). Table -6.

A one-way ANOVA was done with " Get inspired by Graphic Elements" as the independent variable and recoded as Graphic Elements with three groups namely Always,Sometimes and Rarely and dependent variable "Cartoon helps to improve imagination level" is significant.

Table -7 shows $F(3,96)=3.652$; $p=.012$.

A post hoc test was done where children always allow Cartoon character (M=2.11) to understand the feelings through facial expression and those who allows sometimes(M=1.20) and Rarely(M=1.11). Table -6.

T-TEST

3. Watching cartoon helps children to develop their communication skills and influence them in education.

Table-8 Mean

Name of the variable	III std	V std
Get inspired by cartoon characters	1.00	1.22
Get inspired by cartoon visuals	1.00	1.06
Cartoon helps to improve imagination level	1.16	1.06
Cartoon helps to improve verbal communication	2.08	1.08
Cartoon helps to understand subject better than teaching	1.02	1.12

Table-9 Standard Deviation

Name of the variable	III std	V std
Get inspired by cartoon characters	.000	.343
Get inspired by cartoon visuals	.834	1.092
Cartoon helps to improve imagination level	.370	.240
Cartoon helps to improve verbal communication	.853	.274
Cartoon helps to understand subject better than teaching	.141	.328

T test was done with obtained a significant result.

1] III std (M=1.00) is comparatively low comparing with V std (M=1.22) in getting inspired by cartoon characters t(98,49.00)-2.852,p=0.00

2] III std (M=1.00) is comparatively low comparing with V std (M=1.06) in get inspired by cartoon visuals t(98,49.00)-1.769,p=0.00

3] III std (M=1.16) is high comparing with V std (M=1.06) cartoon helps to improve imagination level t(98,83.967)1.603,p=0.001

4] III std (M=2.08) is high comparing with V std (M=1.08) cartoon helps to improve verbal communication t(98,59.001)75.893,p=0.00

5] III std (M=1.02) is comparatively low comparing with V std (M=1.12) cartoons helps to understand subject better than teaching t(98,66.584)18.336,p=0.00

Conclusion from Research Findings

Table -1 shows that respondents out of 100 cases 59% always watches cartoon in their mobile phone. Table -2 says out of 100 cases 63% always watch cartoon for education purpose.Table -3 in the total number of 100 cases 63% always watch cartoon for entertainment. Tables -4 & 5,Cartoon character allows the children to understand the feelings through facial expression.Tables -6&7, indicates Cartoon visuals helps them to create fantasy and improve imagination. Tables 8 & 9 proves that V std students highly getting inspired by cartoon characters, understanding the subject better than teaching and inspired by cartoon visuals than the III std students. III std students were highly improve imagination level and improve verbal communication than V std students by watching cartoon.

Recommendation for Future Research

The finding of this study proves that Watching cartoon helps children to develop their communication skills and it also influence their education.Various cartoon programs help them to create fantasy and it leads to develop their imagination. It helps to understand subject better than teaching where visually they can see, how its functioning, which helps them to understand the concept better. This study on Exposure to Cartoon Programmes and its Impact on School Going Children proves that the V std students are aware of watching cartoon for entertainment equally for education as well than III std students. So this study may help to understand the positive impact of cartoon for the bright future.

References

1. https://www.researchgate.net/publication/344494671 Fantasy Animations and Children's Imagination A Qualitative Study

2. https://www.researchgate.net/publication/345066689 Effect of cartoons on children

3. https://www.academia.edu/44067789/Fantasy Animations and Childrens Imagination A Qualitative Study

4. https://pdf.sciencedirectassets.com/277811/1-s2.0-S1877042812X0017X/1-s2.0-S1877042812017399/main.pdf?X-Amz-Security-5.

5. https://timesofindia.indiatimes.com/life-style/parenting/first-year/watching-cartoons-can-improve-kids-memory-and-narrative-skills-study/articleshow/70482925.cms

6. https://parenting.firstcry.com/articles/positive-and-negative-effects-of-cartoons-on-child-behaviour-and-development/

7. https://www.researchgate.net/publication/323523698 Impact of Cartoon Programs on Children's Language and Behavior

8. https://www.researchgate.net/publication/345066689 Effect of cartoons on children

9. https://www.vanguardngr.com/2019/06/using-cartoons-as-a-learning-and-development-tool-for-children/

10. https://mashandco.tv/en/cartoons-their-importance-in-kids-development/